AUTOBIOGRAPHY of Ek Refugee Scientist

Dr. M.K.Shingari

INDIA • SINGAPORE • MALAYSIA

ISBN

Paperback 979-8-89415-982-9
Hardcase 979-8-89475-266-2

Knowing yourself is the beginning of all wisdom."

– Aristotle

Contents

An Open Letter to the Youth

As I embark on my journey of self-discovery, I found that each reflection was a perfect puzzle piece that brought clarity in my thought process, expanded my vision, changed my perspectives and enlightened me with wisdom.

Youth, today is deserving of the achievements for which they put their efforts in. It gives me an immense pleasure to share with you all my life journey – my own life experiences, converted into the book as a guiding light for today's generation, with an intention of bringing wisdom in their lives through the lessons that I have learned from my life!

You all have the freedom to choose your life goals, to aspire and achieve your goals and to pursue your dreams and passions in today's world. But my time was a little different; today's youth achieve first and then experience, but while I was growing, I had a contrast. I had experiences first and then achievement followed. It came to me as a result of my resilience, hard work and the art of learning from my mistakes.

The flow of my life journey has all the elements in it, from experiencing the traumas of India – Pakistan partition, to the life-changing memories of joining NCC, landing up in foreign lands to earn livelihood, going through the cruel phases of life due to drained financial conditions, seeing betrayals from a close quarter to re-building myself!

So, this book is a live hand holding for you all, navigating you all to understand how life unfolds and how one can sail through it being an inseparable part of it. It has all the drama, twists and turns and still has a genuine and promising learning and optimism to it – as they correctly say, " At the end of the dark tunnel, there is always a light that guides!"

So, I consider it my privilege to share my thrilling life experiences with you all, wishing you all the best as I intent to become a guiding light in your lives and serving you in your life journeys, through my own life experiences, personifying the lessons I learned!

Lastly, I would like to extend my warm wishes to the next generation of India. Be the change you want to see in the environment around you. Become the master of your own authenticity and pursue your dreams with enthusiasm and optimism. There is a bright sunshine waiting for you all! Learn from your experiences and grow to become your best version.

I am really happy to see India transforming into a young nation with its new generation taking the front seat and driving the nation with its innovative thoughts and creative applications of their expertise to bring glory to our nation at a global level!

The nation really wants your able contributions in the various fields and I wish and pray to the Almighty to support you in your endeavors that can bring India pride in more than one way! Keep Shining. God Bless You.

– Dr. M.K. SHINGARI

Foreword

This Autobiography of Dr. Mahender Kumar Shingari is a result of consistent persuasion by my wife and some of his friends. We wanted to write down his journey from a refugee to an Industrialist, at least for the next generations, who otherwise would not realise how bold and far-sighted Dr. Shingari was even from his difficult childhood. He is a person who is focused, has a highly disciplined lifestyle, is a true friend, nature-loving and works for the new goals for his family as well as society. He always says that he works for his satisfaction and doesn't waste time on unnecessary activities. He is a down-to-earth, simple person who never forgets his past and is able to inculcate the same qualities in the next generation.

Ultimately, we were able to pursue him to find time for elaborating his achievements and failure in his 82 years span. Interestingly when he started writing about him, he wrote most of the events in his life within 45 days, a true example of his dedication and commitment.

The readers will get a true insight into a person who started his childhood with refugee parents, starting life from nothing, but he, even as a child, had a wider vision to set his goal of higher study, achieve excellence and convert the knowledge into Indigenous scientific products helping Indian industries including the Indian Nuclear Power Industry. It's really an eye-opener for today's young generation, who can be motivated to face challenges in life with boldness and a positive attitude and finally fulfil their dreams.

The last chapter 'Legacy and Concluding Advice' is the gist of his over 50 years of hard-earned experience and has very useful advice to be followed by the present generation in particular.

I feel very proud to be trusted by Dr. Shingari in contributing to his manuscript. May Almighty God bless him with excellent health and very long life to guide his family, friends and society.

– Girish Kumar Vithal

Introduction

Making a choice with a Voice

"The purpose of life is to be useful, to be honourable, to be compassionate, to have it make some difference that you have lived and lived well."

— Ralph Waldo Emerson

The theme and purpose behind my autobiographical journey stem from two significant events in my life. These events left a profound impact on me, urging me to highlight the themes of injustice, misuse of power and the importance of education. There are two major events of my life that have personified these themes.

Event 1: My First Job after my Graduation

After graduating from Delhi University, I was appointed as a Technical Supervisor at the Central Serum Research Institute (CSRI) in Kasauli, Himachal Pradesh (HP). The Director of the Institute at the time was Mr. J.B. Srivastava, a close associate and confidant of Punjab's Chief Minister, Shri Pratap Singh Kairo.

In 1960s, it was compulsory for employees in all Central Government establishments to learn Hindi. Our Hindi teacher, a young lady of our age, around 21-22 years old, confided in us about the Director's inappropriate behaviour. Being fresh graduates from Delhi University, we engaged in casual conversations about the Director.

Unfortunately, word of our discussions reached the Director, given the fact that Kasauli was a small place. In response, he wielded his considerable influence and suspended all four of us without issuing any show cause notice. Determined to challenge this injustice, we sought legal recourse and obtained a stay order from the district court in Solan.

However, the Director was not deterred by the legal intervention. He leveraged his connections within the Ministry of Health, reaching out to my brother-in-law, Mr. Amar Nath Verma, an Under-secretary in the Health Ministry. Mr. Verma advised us to withdraw the stay order and apologised to the Director, promising to secure alternative employment for us in Delhi or Chandigarh, wherever we preferred. Two of my colleagues accepted positions in Chandigarh, while another secured a job in Delhi. Despite being offered a job in Delhi, I remained steadfast in my decision to continue working at CSRI, Kasauli.

However, my stance was met with resistance from both the Director and my family, ultimately leading to my resignation and return to Delhi. Fortunately, my immediate supervisor at CSRI, Dr. Agarwal, who held a Ph.D. and was affiliated with the Royal Institute of Chemistry, provided me with a commendable certificate, choosing not to mention the aforementioned episode, thus preserving my reputation and integrity.

Major Realisation

I was astonished by the immense authority held by the Director, who possessed only an M.Sc. in Biochemistry, whereas I, with my B.Sc. degree, stood just one qualification below him. This realisation sparked two distinct thoughts in my mind:

1. If a person can be so powerful with an M.Sc. degree, then I should study to go one step above the M.Sc. to become more powerful than the Director.

   or

2. Leave India and migrate to the UK to work & settle there.

Event 2: Hurdles in my way

After facing financial constraints that hindered my pursuit of a postgraduate degree in Biochemistry at various universities across India, I eventually secured admission to the Department of Biochemistry at M.S. University in Baroda.

However, upon assessing the expenses associated with studying for an M.Sc. in Baroda, my family, constrained by limited financial resources and the needs of other dependents, could not support me financially. With my first option falling through, I turned to the British Embassy in New Delhi in search of employment opportunities in England. Surprisingly, I swiftly obtained a work permit to work in the UK for a period of two years, with the possibility of an extension.

Challenges related to my Choices

Despite my efforts, I encountered significant challenges in securing employment in England and Wales that aligned with my educational background, which included a B.Sc. degree from Delhi University. Unfortunately, my degree was not considered equivalent to British qualifications, leading to rejections or offers for menial positions such as a bus conductor, labourer in a chemical factory, or foundry worker. These two pivotal events, one in India and the other in the UK compelled me to prioritise the need to work, earn and save for further education. My strong belief in equality motivated me to strive for higher academic achievements, culminating in obtaining a B.Sc. (Hons) in Chemical Engineering, followed by an M.Sc. and Ph.D. in Engineering.

Upon completing my Ph.D. in Chemical Engineering in the UK, I was offered a lecturer position at the Department of Chemical Engineering at Swansea University. However, my desire to return to my homeland prevailed over staying in the UK.

The Homecoming

After my Ph.D. thesis was accepted by Professor Kene of Cambridge University, with some minor corrections in grammar and spelling, I returned to India in February 1972. I learned about the acceptance of my thesis for Ph.D. work while in India in March 1972 and awaited the formal conferral of the degree at the University's convocation scheduled for July 1972.

My Room in College Hostel

During University Convocation

Meeting the Mentor

During my Ph.D. studies, I had a significant encounter with Mr. Shivaganam, the Principal or Chief Secretary of the Government of Gujarat, who visited our Department of Chemical Engineering. I showcased to him my laboratory, where I was utilising four gas chromatographs to collect data for scaling up from laboratory-scale models to industrial prototype plants. These gas chromatographs were crucial for the separation and manufacture of heat-sensitive compounds on a production scale. Mr. Shivaganam was greatly impressed by our work and encouraged me, along with my colleagues, to return to India and initiate an industry in Gujarat, offering his assistance.

With his help, we obtained land from the Gujarat Industrial Development Corporation in Baroda and secured loans and credit limits from the Bank of Baroda. Motivated by the aim to counteract the brain drain phenomenon and respond to the Government of India's call, I decided to return to my homeland, along with my colleague, Mr. Shrish Bhailal Bhai Patel, who hailed from the Electrical Engineering Department of the same university. Additionally, I encouraged numerous Ph.D. students within my network to come back and contribute to our country's development.

The Partnership

Mr. Shrish Patel and I established our partnership company, Chromatography and Instruments Company, in the GIDC area of Baroda, Gujarat. The name of the company was based on my Ph.D. work in the field of Chromatography. Notably, I constructed two prototype gas chromatographs— one with a single detector and another with dual detectors— designed and assembled with the assistance of technicians from our department. This endeavor was conducted with the approval of my supervisor, Dr. John Condor and the Head of the Chemical Engineering Department, Professor Richardson, who authored numerous volumes of Chemical Engineering textbooks.

Chromatography and Instruments Company continues to thrive, providing employment to over 50 persons of its workforce. Additionally, I am now among the approximately 170,000 individuals out of a population of India - 140 crore who are classified as High Net Individuals, paying more than Rupees one crore as Income Tax.

My Journey as an Example for Others

In this autobiography, I have illustrated how an individual can transform their life through hard work, discipline, vision and unwavering determination. It serves as a testament to my journey from humble beginnings to success, from being an employee to becoming an employer.

Summary

Introduction: Making a Choice with a Voice

Major incidents:

1. First job at the CSRI (Central Serum Research Institute), Kasauli, Himachal Pradesh.
2. Realisation of a strong faith to do something for the motherland.
3. Being classified as a High Net Individual for paying more than Rs. one crore as Income Tax.

Learning:

1. Voices are to be raised fearlessly for the injustice done.
2. Education plays a vital role in establishing an influential position. There will be choices and consequences – so choose wisely!
3. Sometimes rejections are a true blessing in disguise and be open to challenges. Trust the process.
4. The best transformations happen when you work hard, bring discipline, have a vision

(dream) and an unwavering determination to pursue your vision.

Chapter defining quote:

"The effectiveness of earning something becomes valuable only when you know the correct value of putting something equally important at stake against it."

Section 1

The Brutal Face of Fate: The Partition of British India

"Unfolding of a new chapter and tossing the coin for facing the unknown. The independence was acquired, but the heart still bleeds remembering the irrecoverable losses experienced by the families under the heinous act of partition."

Part I: 1947 and the Split of One Nation into Two

In 1947, India bore witness to a profoundly tragic event that would reshape its destiny: the partition of the country into two distinct nations, India and Pakistan. This monumental decision, orchestrated by the British rulers, aimed to address the simmering religious tensions that had long plagued the Indian subcontinent. However, the repercussions of this partition would reverberate far beyond its intended scope, plunging millions into a vortex of chaos, anguish and uncertainty.

The announcement of the partition set off a chain reaction of violence and upheaval. Communal riots erupted in various parts of the country, pitting neighbours against neighbours and sowing seeds of fear and mistrust. The streets became battlegrounds, with innocent lives caught in the crossfire of sectarian strife. Families were torn asunder, with countless lives lost in the carnage that ensued.

India and Pakistan: A Heartbreaking Story of Division and Adversity

The crossing of borders, once symbols of unity, now became harbingers of anguish and despair. Countless souls endured hunger, sickness and hardship as they traversed vast distances on foot, their spirits weighed down by the Specter of loss and displacement. The lack of clear demarcation only added to the confusion, leaving many stranded in limbo, unsure of where they truly belonged.

Amidst the chaos and violence of the partition, women and children found themselves disproportionately affected, bearing the heaviest burdens of the turmoil. Women endured unspeakable acts of violence and abuse, becoming victims of the widespread atrocities that ravaged communities. Meanwhile, children were orphaned in staggering numbers and left to navigate the harsh realities of a world torn apart by conflict. Families were torn asunder, their bonds shattered by the unforgiving tide of history, leaving behind a legacy of pain, suffering and irreparable loss.

In conclusion, the partition of India and Pakistan stands as a somber testament to the devastating consequences of communal division and political upheaval. The rapid and tumultuous nature of the partition led to a mass exodus of unprecedented scale, with millions of Hindus, Sikhs and Muslims uprooted from their homes and forced to seek refuge across hastily drawn borders. The toll number of lives lost ranging from hundreds of thousands to millions exacted by this traumatic event was staggering, with estimates of the number of lives lost ranging from hundreds of thousands to millions.

A life-changing moment in my life

Where we became destitute refugees from landowners overnight!

Within my own family, the partition exacted a heavy toll, leaving us bereft of our ancestral lands and livelihoods. Hailing from Chak Jhumra in East Punjab on my father's side and Mirakpur in East Punjab on my mother's side, our once-prosperous existence was irrevocably shattered by the partition. Overnight, we went from being landowners to destitute refugees, reliant on the goodwill of the Indian Government for our survival. The scars of the partition continue to linger, a painful reminder of the profound upheaval brought by this tragic chapter in history.

Displacement looks Cruel when Applied Forcibly

The migration from Pakistan to India stands as a tumultuous and heart-wrenching chapter in the histories of both my paternal and maternal families, echoing the broader upheaval and suffering experienced by millions during the partition. The partition of British India in 1947, driven by religious divisions, unleashed a wave of violence and chaos that reverberated across the subcontinent. The catastrophic aftermath of this division saw the displacement of millions, accompanied by a staggering death toll that surpassed 600,000 lives lost. Muslims, Hindus, Sikhs and others found themselves caught in the crossfire of communal violence, forced to flee their homes in search of safety and refuge. Whatever I gathered initially from my parents and uncles, I am trying to script it about how my paternal and maternal grandfathers struggled to get settled in India after crossing the border.

Amidst the turmoil, my family faced the agonising decision to leave their ancestral homeland in Punjab, Pakistan, for the uncertain shores of East Punjab, India. While some families opted to stay behind, clinging to hope amidst the chaos, others, including my own, made the perilous journey across the border in search of sanctuary. Given my grandfather's prominent position as the Station House officer in the area, a Muslim friend extended a lifeline of safety by offering refuge in his home.

This act of kindness proved crucial in ensuring my family's survival, especially when false reports of their demise circulated, prompting a daring rescue mission led by my uncle, Major Pran Nath Sarin.

From Mirakpur to the Lahore base camp, Major Pran Nath orchestrated the family's safe passage, navigating treacherous terrain and evading danger at every turn. His efforts culminated in the reunion of scattered family members, including my grandparents, parents, uncles and aunts, in the relative safety of Lahore.

Part II: Re-building Life in an Unfamiliar Territory

The arduous journey continued as the family embarked on the daunting task of crossing the border, braving unimaginable hardships and deprivation along the way. Their odyssey took them through Refugee Camps in Derababa Nanak, Ramdas and Gurdaspur, where they encountered further trials, including exploitation at the hands of unscrupulous individuals like Dr. Bhagat Ram. Despite finding temporary shelter in Refugee Camps in Jalandhar Cantt, their respite was short-lived as natural disasters, such as floods, struck with devastating consequences. Forced to relocate once again, the family found themselves dispersed, with some members settling in Aligarh under the guidance of Nana's Muslim friend, while others made their home in Delhi, marking the beginning of a new chapter fraught with uncertainty and challenges.

This dangerous journey, marked by displacement, loss and survival, etched an indelible chapter in the history of my family's endurance and resilience during the partition from Pakistan to India.

Aligarh and Delhi - One Family with Two Fates

My Nana and his entire family moved to Aligarh and my Dada's family moved to Delhi. Life at both these places unfolds differently for all of us; let me take you on a tour describing the same.

Aligarh Becomes a New Chapter in my Maternal Family.

Following their migration, my maternal grandfather, fondly referred to as Nana, alongside his family comprising four sons and two daughters, settled in Aligarh, located approximately 150 kilometers(km) from Delhi. Upon their arrival in Aligarh, they found shelter in a sizeable, deserted structure previously occupied by migrated Muslims. This structure, known locally as *Punjabiyo ki Kothi (House of Punjabis)* on Gular Road, served multiple functions—it functioned as a warehouse and a factory and was surrounded by several smaller residential units within the compound, accommodating around 70 to 80 individuals. My Nana's family was allocated the largest quarter within this complex, consisting of five rooms, a kitchen and a solitary bathroom. Among Nana's sons, the eldest, Mr. Balwant Raj Sarin, armed with an M.A. in English, secured a lecturer position in the English Department at Dharam Smaj Degree College. The second son, Dr. Harbans Raj Sarin, a qualified doctor, began working at a small Government Hospital on a temporary basis, earning a modest income. The third son, Mr. Ranbir Singh Sarin, ventured to a village called Dadon, located 40 km away from Aligarh City, where he inherited a significant parcel of agricultural land previously owned by a Muslim farmer who had migrated to Pakistan. Meanwhile, the youngest son, Mr. Vishwa Nath Sarin, assumed the role of managing the household and family affairs, albeit without being actively engaged in any specific occupation.

A wish dear to the heart

Prior to his demise, Nana expressed a poignant wish to his sons—that upon his passing, he wished to be cremated in Punjab, his ancestral land. Unfortunately, in 1953, he suffered a fatal heart attack while visiting a friend in Ramdas Town and breathed his last there. True to his wishes, he was cremated in Punjab as per his final request. In the absence of young children in the household, Nana's family collectively decided to bring one child from their eldest daughter's family, who resided in Delhi. As the fourth child,

I was chosen and brought to Aligarh, where I remained until completing my high school education. Only thereafter did I relocate to Delhi with my parents.

Delhi Becomes a New Chapter in my Paternal Family

Initially, upon their migration, my paternal grandfather, accompanied by his three sons and two daughters, found themselves among a few refugees seeking shelter in Sabji Mandi locality in Delhi. However, after a short while, they relocated to an old building vacated by Muslims in the same area. As time passed, certain members of the family decided to settle in different neighbourhoods within Delhi. Some opted for the Ashram locality in Lajpat Nagar-1 as their new residence, while others chose a double-story house in Lajpat Nagar-4. Additionally, a few family members settled in Amar Colony, also situated in Lajpat Nagar, New Delhi.

For a period, all members of the family resided at the Ashram until the Government provided a small quarter for their family after several months. This modest dwelling became their new home. Subsequently, my grandfather's family transitioned to this allocated quarter in Lajpat Nagar-2, signifying a shift to a more stable living situation compared to the earlier temporary arrangements in various locations within Delhi.

Rehabilitation and Grants for Displaced People

Following the mass migration from Pakistan, refugees encountered immediate and daunting challenges spanning housing, financial stability, employment, education and healthcare. Recognising the urgent needs of these displaced individuals, the Indian Government took proactive measures to provide rehabilitation and grants, aiming to assist them in re-building their shattered lives.

To facilitate this assistance, the Central Government appointed various officials, including Settlement Commissioners, tasked with evaluating compensation and grants for the refugees. These displaced persons were required to complete and submit applications outlining their verified claims for compensation within a specified timeframe, often three months from the date mentioned in the Official Gazette. As the head of our family, the responsibility to complete the compensation application fell upon my father. However, due to limited educational attainment, my father and his brother sought assistance from other refugees residing in the camps to navigate the application process.

In an effort to expedite the proceedings and obtain essential resources promptly, our family consciously opted to claim compensation solely for housing and business premises. This strategic decision involved focusing on minimal amounts, ensuring a swift approval process. The primary objective behind this approach was to promptly secure immediate shelter for the family, facilitating their transition out of the refugee camp and into the Ashram locality. This deliberate step aimed to establish a more stable and conducive living environment for our family amidst the challenges posed by displacement.

The Tale of Meher Chand Refugee Market, Lodhi Road

Following our stay at the Ashram, the Government allotted us a 100-square-metre house, providing accommodation with two bedrooms—one for my father's family and another for my youngest uncle's family. However, this allocation initially overlooked lodging for my another uncle's family. Through persistent appeals and efforts, authorities eventually arranged a room for them at Lodhi Road Barracks, ensuring accommodation for the entire family unit.

Concurrently, the Government initiated the construction of markets comprising 100 shops each. Upon submission of our compensation application, my father and one uncle were fortunate to receive shops at the "Meher Chand Refugee Market" located at Lodhi Road. Similarly, the third uncle obtained a shop at the Raj Kumari Amrit Kaur market at Karbala, Lodhi Road.

During our migration, our family had brought along some gold and silver jewelry, which we sold to establish a grocery shop. Subsequently, we diversified into managing a ration depot, a concession specifically allotted to my youngest uncle. These initiatives, facilitated by the Government, laid the groundwork for us to embark on a dignified livelihood. The steadfast assistance provided by the Government played a pivotal role in enabling our family to sustain ourselves independently. It freed us from reliance on charity and served as a testament to the invaluable support we received during the trying and challenging phase of our lives. We are deeply grateful to the Government for its aid, which empowered us to forge our path toward self-reliance and prosperity.

Summary

Section 1: The Brutal Face of Fate: The Partition of British India

Major incidents:

1. Migration from ancestral lands into an unfamiliar territory and having to rebuild again. The family was divided as well.

Learning:

1. Dislocations can bring challenges, but if one is true to one's roots, then one can still sail through in the toughest times.
2. The strength is to stand together in every thick and thin situations.

Chapter defining quote:

"I was inexperienced and the life's canvas was new, so I chose to explore the new possibilities within it to mark the beginning of a true masterpiece."

Section 2

Family: The First Foundation in Life

"A tree that spreads wisdom to all its generations."

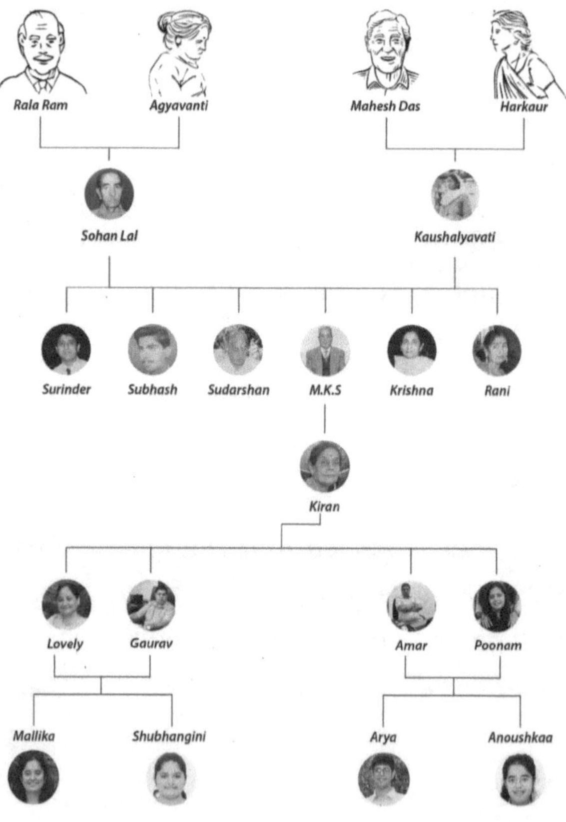

Part I: Paternal Grandfather - *"Hamare Pyare Dada ji"*

Family is the 1st Milestone

My paternal grandfather, affectionately known as Dada, led a prosperous life in Chak Jhumra, District – Lyallpur. He was engaged in wholesale grain trading and money lending, building a successful livelihood for his family. However, his life took a significant turn when he lost his sight in 1938, at the age of 75, while my grandmother (Dadi) was around 60 years old. Despite this challenge, Dada remained resilient and continued to navigate life with determination and strength.

Dada and Dadi were blessed with three sons and three daughters, forming a close-knit family unit. Despite the loss of his sight, Dada remained an integral part of his family's life, providing guidance and support to his children and grandchildren. His wisdom and values served as pillars for the family, shaping their character and outlook on life.

The Rich Legacy of Dada & Dadi Ji

"The one who comes to life has to depart one day; it is the body that departs, but the valuable legacy is re-lived forever."

In 1962, at the remarkable age of 99, Dada passed away, leaving behind a legacy of hard work, resilience and love. His passing marked the end of an era for the family as they mourned the loss of their patriarch. Despite the challenges they faced, Dada's teachings and principles continued to guide them through life's trials and tribulations.

Following Dada's demise, the family experienced another tragedy with Dadi's passing in 1963, just a year later. Her loss was deeply felt by all, as she had been the matriarch of the family, providing love, care and support to her children and grandchildren. Despite the sorrow of losing both their grandparents within a short span, the family found solace in the memories and values instilled by Dada and Dadi.

Additionally, the family endured another heartbreaking loss in 1963 with the passing of my mother. Her absence left a void in the family, as she had been a source of love, warmth and guidance to her children. The collective grief of losing three beloved family members within a year was a profound challenge for the family to overcome.

This is What my Paternal Family looks like

Here are the details of my family members from the Paternal side, each contributing to the rich tapestry of our family history and legacy:

- Paternal Grandfather (Dada)
- Paternal Grandmother (Dadi)
- Three Sons
- Three Daughters

1. **My father - Completed 8th grade**
2. **My uncle 1- Completed 8th grade**
3. **My uncle 2 - Completed 7th grade**

My father and both uncles acquired valuable experience in managing wholesale grain trading, a business they inherited from our paternal grandfather, Dada. Additionally, uncle 2 specialised in the money lending business, expanding the family's financial ventures. Despite the challenges posed by the partition of India in 1947, all three brothers successfully navigated their way through the upheaval, starting as shopkeepers and managing to sustain a reasonable standard of living. My father, Shri Sohanlal ji, held the esteemed position of being the eldest son in the family, with his younger brothers, Shri Mulkh Raj and Shri Bhua Das, following in birth order. Together, my father and my youngest uncle, Shri Bhua Das, ventured into the grocery shop and ration depot business, leveraging their collective expertise and determination to carve out a livelihood for themselves and their families.

Tragically, the passage of time had brought sorrow and loss to our family. My uncles passed away in Delhi due to natural causes. Despite leading fulfilling lives, they bid farewell to this world, leaving behind cherished memories and a lasting legacy of hard work and resilience.

Furthermore, the passage of time has seen the loss of all the members of my uncles' families as well. Their absence serves as a poignant reminder of the transient nature of life and the importance of cherishing every moment spent with loved ones.

As for my own family, we, too, have experienced the pain of loss. My father, in particular, met his end in a road accident at the age of 94, marking a sudden and unexpected departure from our lives. Both my elder sisters passed away, with one in Delhi in the year 2022 and the other in the UK in the year 2023.

Their departures have left an indelible mark on our hearts, as we fondly remember the love, laughter and joy they brought into our lives. Though they may no longer be with us in person, their spirits live on in our cherished memories and the bonds of love that continue to bind our family together.

Part II: Maternal Grandfather - "*Hamare Pyare Nana Ji*"

A notable contribution to raise the family and making them responsible

In a parallel narrative, the story of my maternal grandfather, fondly known as Nana, unfolds amidst significant challenges and responsibilities. Residing in Mirakpur, situated in District Narowal, Nana, whose official title was Shri Mahesh Shaji, held a position of great esteem as a Zaildar. This role bestowed upon him various administrative duties and financial responsibilities within the community. As the Zaildar, Nana was tasked with overseeing the collection of revenue for the British Government, a duty that earned him a salary equivalent to 1% of the revenue he collected.

Despite the weight of his responsibilities, the support provided by the British Government was minimal, limited to a horse and a solitary helper to aid him in his tasks.

The role of my Nana Ji is that of a Devoted Family Man!

Alongside his esteemed position as Zaildar, Nana was a devoted family man, blessed with four sons, each with their own unique educational background and two daughters. His role as an Administrator cum Finance Minister demanded meticulous attention to detail and unwavering dedication to his duties. Beyond the bureaucratic demands of his position, Nana's commitment to his family remained unwavering as he strived to provide for their needs and ensure their well-being amidst the challenges of the times.

The duties of a Zaildar were multifaceted, encompassing not only the collection of revenue but also the maintenance of law and order within the community. Nana's authority extended beyond mere administrative tasks; he was a pillar of strength and guidance for the people under his jurisdiction. Despite the limited resources at his disposal, Nana discharged his duties with integrity and diligence, earning the respect and admiration of those around him.

Mirkapur's Story from Calm to Turmoil

However, the idyllic tranquility of Mirakpur was soon shattered by the tumultuous events of the partition of India in 1947. Like countless others, Nana and his family found themselves engulfed in the chaos and uncertainty that accompanied the partition. The once-peaceful streets of

Mirakpur became fraught with tension and fear as communal violence erupted, tearing apart the fabric of society and leaving families displaced and disoriented.

Amidst the turmoil, Nana faced the daunting task of ensuring the safety and security of his family amidst the escalating violence. With the partition looming large, Nana was confronted with difficult choices and agonising decisions as he grappled with the uncertain future that lay ahead. Despite the overwhelming challenges, Nana remained steadfast in his resolve, drawing upon his inner strength and resilience to navigate through the turbulent waters of history.

This is what my Maternal Family looks like

Here are the details of my maternal uncles

1. Eldest uncle - Shri Balwant Raj Sarin, an M.A. in English, held the prestigious position of a professor at Aligarh.
2. Second uncle - Dr. Hansraj Sarin established a clinic in Aligarh.
3. Thakur Ragbir Singh - Possessed a B.A. degree and was a significant landlord managing a dairy farm in Dado, Aligarh.

4. Vishwa Nath Sarin - Attained up to the 12th grade but did not succeed. He led a middle-class life, working as a farmer in Aligarh City.

'Education' - the Biggest Legacy of my Maternal Family

The educational achievements of all my maternal uncles affectionately referred to as "Mamas," were notably impressive and contributed significantly to our family's legacy. Each uncle pursued education beyond the school level, acquiring substantial knowledge and expertise in their respective fields. Their commitment to learning and personal growth served as a source of inspiration for future generations, instilling values of diligence and academic excellence within our family. Conversely, my maternal aunt, fondly known as "Masi" and my mother received education only up to the school level. While their educational journey may have been comparatively shorter, their contributions to the family were equally significant.

Despite not pursuing higher education, my mother and my masi played vital roles in nurturing and supporting their families, imparting invaluable life lessons and fostering a sense of unity and resilience within our family unit. Today, all my maternal uncles and aunt have passed away, leaving behind a rich legacy of diverse accomplishments and educational achievements. Their collective contributions have greatly influenced our family's history, shaping our values, aspirations and sense of identity. As we reflect on their lives and accomplishments, we honour them in memory and celebrate the lasting impact they have had on our family's journey.

Part III: Only a Strong Culture Can Build a Good Human Being

"The cultural abundance that I inherited from both sides of my family has shaped me into what I am today."

The Hindu Culture: A Rich Tapestry Indeed

Hindu culture is a vibrant tapestry woven with traditions, beliefs, rituals and values that have stood the test of time, influencing the lives of millions worldwide. Immersed in this ancient heritage, I am deeply connected to its essence, cherishing its teachings and embracing its richness. Belonging to the Hindu culture fills me with pride as I carry forward its rich legacy. Rooted in spirituality, compassion and morality, Hinduism encompasses a vast spectrum of philosophical beliefs and practices. From the wisdom of the Vedas, Upanishads and Bhagavad Gita to the timeless epics like the Ramayana and Mahabharata, our sacred texts serve as guiding beacons for spiritual seekers and moral compasses for ethical living.

As a member of the Punjabi community, I inherit a heritage steeped in valor, integrity and honour, tracing back to the esteemed Kshatriya lineage. Historically known as warriors and administrators, the Kshatriyas embody courage and resilience, passing down a legacy of diligence, strength and leadership through generations.

Education stands as a cornerstone of our family's identity, reflecting our commitment to knowledge and personal growth. In alignment with Hindu culture, which venerates wisdom and enlightenment, we recognise education as a catalyst for societal progress and individual fulfilment.

Within our familial sphere, the esteemed ladies epitomise the heart and soul of our traditions. Embracing religious devotion and spiritual values, they embody compassion, strength and resilience. Their choice of vegetarianism reflects our reverence for life and echoes the principle of ahinsa, advocating non-violence and compassion towards all living beings. The religious fervor within our family serves as a powerful bond, uniting us through shared rituals, prayers and celebrations. Festivals like Lohri, Diwali, Holi and Navratri bring us together, infusing our lives with joy, spiritual devotion and a profound sense of community. These occasions create lasting connections that span across generations, strengthening the fabric of our familial ties.

Our revered ladies uphold traditions by faithfully observing fasts during auspicious periods such as Navratri, Janmashtami and Karva Chauth. These rituals, undertaken with devotion and dedication, are not only acts of faith but also symbols of love and commitment within our family.

It's worth noting that I have personally contributed to our religious practices by constructing two temples. The first temple, located in Baroda, as a tribute to my revered mother, holds personal significance, while the second temple stands in Solan along NH-5, dedicated to my beloved father, serving the public. Renowned in Himachal Pradesh, this temple is distinguished by its unique design, featuring five stories at the foothills of the Himalayas. The temple stands as a testament to our devotion and reverence for spirituality, embodying our family's deep-rooted connection to our religious heritage. Photographs of this magnificent temple capture its grandeur and significance in our lives.

BARODA TEMPLE

This temple is built in the memory of my Mother-

Smt. Kaushalya Devi

SOLAN TEMPLE

This temple is built in the memory of my Father-

Shri Sohan Lal Shingari

In addition to the construction of two temples, I have undertaken the creation of Sohan Lal (*Father*) Hall and Kaushalyavati (*Mother*) Hall within the Doctor & Doctor complex in Baroda, in honour of their cherished memories. These halls serve not only as physical structures but also as symbolic representations of the values and legacies instilled by my parents.

The utilisation of these halls extends beyond mere occupancy, as they are leased out to various companies. The rental income generated from these establishments serves a noble purpose—it is directed towards Dr. Shingari Charitable Trust.

The Trust for a Noble Cause: Dr. Shingari Charitable Trust

At the age of 56 years, I formed Dr. Shingari Charitable Trust in January 1998. The purpose of the trust is to promote education through financial help to needy and deserving persons.

The other purpose is to support deserving persons needing medical treatment. Trust is created for the benefit of persons without any distinction of cast, colour, creed, or religion. Our trust was registered with Charitable Commissioner Vadodara via registration no. E/267/Vadodara Dt. 03.02.1998 and also got permission under Section 15G for exemption and relief, as per the act, to claim a rebate in income tax to the donors to the trust for the financial year 1999-2000. After the expiry of the first year of Tax Exemption, we applied to the Commissioner Income Tax for the renewal of exemption under Section 15G for further five years.

Our application for the renewal was rejected because we refused to entertain the Income Tax Officer. To date, no one outside the Shingari family has donated anything to the trust. This trust is running with the original Corpus (Trust Fund).

The Trust is Truly a Guiding Light for the Students.

The Trust sponsors the expenses for school going children up to 12th Standard only. It has so far funded nine students and some of them have completed their professional degrees and are well settled. One of our sponsored children, is in a very good position in USA. Apart from education, the trust has helped many needy persons for the medical treatments in Baroda as well as in Solan, Himachal Pradesh.

A culture that serves for the greatest cause of humanity

In conclusion, Hindu culture serves as a magnificent embodiment of diversity, spirituality and timeless wisdom. Its rich tapestry, intricately woven with threads of tradition, philosophy and values, offers a profound sense of identity and purpose to its adherents. As someone deeply immersed in this cultural heritage, I hold a deep appreciation for its teachings, finding profound resonance in its philosophies while embracing the richness it adds to my life's journey.

The depth and breadth of Hindu culture are awe-inspiring, spanning thousands of years and encompassing a vast array of beliefs, rituals and practices. From the ancient wisdom found in sacred texts like the Vedas and Upanishads to the colourful celebrations of festivals like Diwali and Holi, Hindu culture reflects the multifaceted nature of human existence.

At its core, Hinduism teaches principles of compassion, righteousness and spiritual growth.

It encourages individuals to seek enlightenment through self-discovery and introspection, guiding them on a path towards inner peace and fulfilment. These timeless teachings resonate with people of all ages and backgrounds, offering solace and guidance in times of joy and adversity alike.

As a proud participant in this cultural legacy, I find myself continuously inspired by the profound truths and universal values espoused by Hinduism. Its emphasis on harmony with nature, respect for all living beings and pursuit of knowledge resonates deeply with my own beliefs and aspirations. Through embracing these teachings, I strive to lead a life guided by integrity, compassion and spiritual awareness, thereby enriching my journey and contributing positively to the world around me.

Part IV: Bachpan aur Bachpan Ke Din

"Childhood is truly a bliss; it's the first step to learn and grow."

My Schooling and Childhood Days

As recounted earlier, during my stay with my maternal grandfather, Nana and his extended family in Aligarh, I was around 5½ years old. It was during this time that my uncles took the proactive step of enrolling me in a modest primary school in the year 1948. This educational institution, overseen and managed by a Pandit Ji, had a rather unconventional set-up. Instead of a conventional building, the school operated under the expansive shade of a large neem tree located at the "chopal" and dairy farm owned by a prominent landlord known as Choudhry Ji. Remarkably, this tree served as the classroom for our early education.

Situated just 600 to 700 meters from our residence, the school's proximity made it easily accessible, requiring only a short journey across a single field(*khet*). Despite its humble surroundings, this unassuming primary school played a vital role in laying the groundwork for my academic journey. The sprawling branches of the neem tree provided a tranquil and conducive environment for learning, where we absorbed the lessons of language, mathematics and more under the open sky. Despite lacking the conventional infrastructure of a typical school, this makeshift set-up fostered a sense of camaraderie and community among the students. We forged bonds with our peers as we sat together on the ground, eagerly absorbing the knowledge imparted by our dedicated Pandit Ji. The simplicity of the set-up belied the significance of the education we received, instilling in us a thirst for knowledge and a love for learning that would accompany us throughout our lives.

1ST Milestone of my School - Primary Education

Remembering my 1st Encounter with Pandit Ji

In the year 1948, my journey through formal education commenced as I took my first steps into primary school. The headmaster, who doubled as our teacher, left a lasting impression with his strict demeanor and unwavering disciplinary measures. Renowned for his short temper and intolerance for even the slightest errors, he employed a slender stick known as *'Kalicharan,'* crafted from neem wood, to administer punishment.

Of paramount importance to our headmaster was proficiency in writing and the memorisation of multiplication tables. Punctuality was non-negotiable in his classroom, with tardiness of as little as ten minutes resulting in ten strikes from the '*dandi.*' Absences incurred the punishment of "*murga*", where the student summed a specific posture for a designated period as a penalty. Our early lessons commenced with the rudimentary task of writing alphabets and numbers on wooden planks called "*takhthi.*" Using ink and pens fashioned from branches of the "*kaana*" plant, known for its supple nature, we diligently practised under the guidance of our teacher. Once the *takhthi* was filled, it was washed and special clay was applied on it to be used next day.

Upon mastering handwriting basics, we transitioned to "*slates*". To meticulously practice alphabets and numerals on both sides. This routine honed our skills and fostered familiarity with Hindi and English alphabets. Numerical exercises conducted in English contributed significantly to our educational foundation during those early school years.

My 1st mischievous Act in Pandit Ji's Class

Recollections from my elders depict me as a mischievous child during my formative schooling years, often at odds with our stern headmaster, Pandit Ji. Known for his volatile temper and authoritarian approach, he seemed to relish disciplining us. Consequently, a pervasive sense of fear and trepidation hung over us in his presence. Pandit Ji's teaching sessions were relentless, sparing no breaks—no holidays, not even Sundays. One particular incident remains etched in my memory, emblematic of Pandit Ji's fiery temperament. During a class, when a student expressed difficulty in seeing the blackboard, I made a quip about Pandit Ji being irreplaceable as the writer.

Unfortunately, he caught wind of my remark and promptly called me forward. Sensing trouble, I fled the school premises with my slate and belongings. Enraged by my escape, Pandit Ji hurled the slate at me, causing injury. Hastening home, I recounted the incident to my maternal uncle (*Mama Ji*), seeking comfort. Instead, I was reprimanded and made to stand, holding my ears, under the assumption that I must have provoked Pandit Ji's wrath.

Following the distressing incident, my aversion to returning to school was resolute. However, my uncle intervened, urging me to extend an apology to Pandit Ji for my actions. Surprisingly,

Pandit Ji received my apology with grace, assuring me of a cessation of physical punishment in the future. Despite my initial reluctance, I had little recourse but to resume my education under Pandit Ji's tutelage.

In hindsight, I've come to appreciate Pandit Ji's proficiency and dedication as an educator. It was under his guidance that my penmanship flourished and my aptitude for mathematics markedly improved. His influence instilled in me a sense of discipline that has served me well throughout my life. The memory of my first teacher remains vivid in my mind and I hold him in high regard. Reflecting on my educational journey, I am deeply thankful for his teachings, which left an enduring impact on my life.

My education under Pandit Ji's stewardship continued until the culmination of my 5th standard, marking the end of an era characterised by growth, learning and the guidance of a remarkable teacher.

Part V: My Journey towards the High School Secondary Education (Up to 10th Class)

The Journey to the Inter College

Transitioning from the rudimentary education offered under the neem tree to Dharam Smaj Inter College marked a pivotal moment in my academic journey. This shift occurred when I entered the 6th standard on the 10th of June 1952. The meticulous arrangements for this transition were spearheaded by my uncle, who assumed the responsibility of enrolling me in this institution. An intriguing aspect arose during the admission process when, inadvertently, my uncle recorded my date of birth as the 7th of June 1942, instead of my actual birth date, the 1st of November 1941. This clerical discrepancy persisted across all official documents and certificates while our family consistently commemorated and acknowledged my birthday on the 1st of November.

All about Dharamsmaj Inter College

Located approximately 3 km from our residence, DharamSmaj Inter College adhered to a daily schedule commencing at 8 A.M. to 1 P.M. in summer and 9 A.M. to 2 P.M. in winter. Despite varying weather conditions, I embarked on the daily journey to school on foot. As a refugee with extremely limited resources, I possessed only two sets of clothing, comprising two pairs of half-pants (*Nikkar*), two shirts, two vests (*khadi baniyan)* and a single pair of shoes. These meagre resources were expected to last the entire year, with replacements provided only during the Diwali festival.

The management of my clothing necessitated a collaborative effort involving my younger maternal aunt (*Mami*), who diligently was head and arranging my clothing to be ironed by an outside Dhobi residing approximately 2 km away in a small hut within a dense jungle. Typically, the Dhobi would deliver the ironed clothes; however, on occasions when he failed to do so, we had to retrieve them from his residence cum shop.

At school, I forged friendships with numerous boys of similar age, hailing from diverse religious backgrounds, such as Hindu and Sikh. Our camaraderie blossomed over mischievous escapades, including ventures into fields to clandestinely savors fruits like *Kakari*, Cucumber, Watermelon, Muskmelon and the pilfering of fruits like Jamphal (*Amrud*), Mangoes and Raspberries from gardens. Our mischievous exploits often resulted in reprimands and occasional beatings from farmers and landowners who caught us in the act. Eventually, complaints reached our homes regarding these activities, prompting apologies and promise not to repeat the offences, which somewhat curtailed our adventures. Nonetheless, occasional relapses occurred, with our group gaining notoriety for engaging in such mischief.

Recalling a Mischievous Incident from Class 7th

I vividly recall a particular incident from my time in the 7th class at school, which left a lasting impression on me. Known for my friendly and occasionally mischievous nature, I found myself at odds with a boy in my class who was considerably taller than me and persistently teased and annoyed me. Despite my complaints to the teacher, his behaviour persisted, escalating my frustration.

These boys ported along plaited tuft of hair, known as "*bodi*," a customary style among Pundits. Seeking retaliation for his persistent teasing, I confided in my youngest uncle, who suggested I pull the boy's tuft as a form of retribution.

One day, during our school prayer session, the boy began pinching and irritating me once again, pushing me to my breaking point. In a fit of anger, I seized his tuft with both hands, jumping up and inadvertently pulling it so hard that it came loose, causing his head to bleed. His cries drew the attention of the teacher, who promptly intervened and brought me, along with several other boys, to the Principal's office.

Faced with the threat of expulsion and the demand for my parents' presence, I confided in my *Mama Ji,* who informed his elder brother, Professor Balwant Raj, a faculty member at the college associated with our school. Accompanied by my eldest *Mama Ji,* we confronted the Principal, where I recounted my version of events. Amidst the turmoil, my *Mama Ji* reprimanded me by slapping me multiple times, pledging to monitor the situation closely.

Gradually, I realised the need to amend my behaviour, although it proved to be a challenging endeavor.

The Role of the RSS as my Savior (Rashtriya Swayamsevak Sangh)

In an effort to channel my energy positively, I joined the Rashtriya Swayamsevak Sangh (RSS) to learn self-defence techniques. Attending RSS sessions became a regular part of my routine, commencing every morning at 5:30 A.M. Additionally, I actively participated in various school activities such as cricket, kabaddi, guidance and playing marbles (*Kanchas*) outside the school premises.

Despite my *Mamaji's* periodic disciplinary measures to ensure I devoted ample time to study, my academic performance remained average, hovering around 55% mark throughout my high school years till the 10th standard. Despite my efforts, I could not secure a first class ranking, consistently landing in the upper second class, between 50% and 56%. Eventually, I completed my 10th-grade education, attaining a second-division pass from the U.P. Board.

My curiosity about "*Bhoot*" & "*Chudels*"

During my 8th to 10th grade, I became intrigued by tales of ghosts ("*Bhoot*") and a female spirit known as "*Chudel*," characterised by long white hair. These eerie and frightening stories captured my imagination, leading to a fascination with the supernatural. Our joint family often slept outside on the veranda due to inadequate lighting inside the house, relying primarily on kerosene lamps known as "*lalten*". The garden surrounding our home, with its large trees, added to the ambience. On windy nights, the rustling of these trees, coupled with flashlight beams from passersby, created peculiar shadowy images resembling ghosts and spirits among the leaves, intensifying the eerie sensation. This sense of intrigue and fascination persisted throughout my time in Aligarh, shaping my perspective on the supernatural. Allow me to recount an incident involving my perceived encounter with a *Chudel* or *Bhootni*.

Second Memorable Incident about the *Chudel*

In the year 1955, when I was approximately 13 years old, our family faced the challenge of having only two sets of clothes for each person. One set was worn while the other was sent for ironing to a local presser. On a particular day, the presser failed to return our clothes as promised. Consequently, I was tasked with retrieving them from his residence, which lay beyond a dense jungle roughly 2 km away from our house. Setting out around 5:30 P.M. I traversed the jungle to reach his place.

However, upon arrival, I discovered that our clothes hadn't been ironed, necessitating a wait. By the time I received the clothes, darkness had already descended. With tales of evil spirits like *Bhoot Pret* and *Chudel* haunting the jungle looming large in my mind, I felt an overwhelming sense of anxiety. Friends had advised chanting a protective prayer to God Hanuman Ji to ward off these spirits, so I recited *"Bhoot Pishaach Nikat Nahi Aave, Mahaveer Jab Naam Sunaave"* as I made my way through the jungle, internally fearful yet resolute in my determination to proceed.

While traversing the path, I suddenly caught sight of an old lady clad in white attire with long white hair seated at a distance. Trembling with fear, I continued chanting the protective prayer, but I couldn't muster the courage to approach her. Instead, I remained frozen, torn between fear and curiosity. In our friend circle, there was a belief that one could control a *Chudel* (Witch) by grabbing her hair, thereby obtaining anything desired. Despite entertaining this notion, I couldn't bring myself to act upon it. After a while, the old lady vanished from sight, leaving me bewildered and even more apprehensive. Summoning what little courage I had left, I hurried along the path, continuing to chant the protective prayer, all the while full of fear.

Upon reaching my maternal uncle and aunt's place, they greeted me with concern and scolded me for my tardiness. They cautioned me against waiting at the presser's place and emphasised the dangers of traversing through the jungle at night. Reflecting on my experience, I realised the gravity of my mistake.

Impact of Shri Rabindranath Tagore on my Life

Approximately a year later, I stumbled upon a book by Nobel Laureate Rabindranath Tagore, where he elucidated that during childhood, imaginative thoughts might seem real and influence our thought processes, particularly during hormonal changes. This revelation prompted me to contemplate whether my fear of evil spirits, as well as the sighting of the old lady in white, were merely figments of my imagination or if there had indeed been a tangible presence that I had encountered.

Tagore's book imparted a profound lesson that left an indelible mark on my character—the discomfort that accompanies conscious wrongdoing.

This realisation has since guided my commitment to unwavering honesty, regardless of the situation. I have made it a personal mandate to always speak the truth and if, inadvertently, I utter something incorrect, I swiftly rectify my mistake and offer an apology. This principle has seamlessly woven itself into the fabric of my being, shaping my conduct and interactions with others.

I attribute this moral compass to the wisdom imparted by Nobel Laureate Rabindranath Tagore, whose teachings continue to resonate deeply within me, influencing my ethical framework and guiding my actions.

Summary

Section 2: Family - The First Foundation in Life

Major incidents:

1. Re-building the careers! – Managing the households with responsibility. Education is the foremost step towards the development and growth.
2. The Hindu culture and its rich legacy.
3. From re-building for the family to re-building for the social cause! – The Shingari Trust.
4. Childhood learnings under Pandit Ji's guidance and higher education lessons.
5. A transitional change in the academic journey (From neem Tree *Gurukul* to a sophisticated college).
6. Joining the RSS – as a tool to vent off the buried frustrations!

Learning:

1. There is always a hidden learning – whether it is sitting under a neem tree or studying in a good college.

2. The essence of understanding the approach to living life comes from reading and understanding the works of a renowned artist, educationist and philosopher.

Chapter defining quote:

"Let my thoughts come to you when I am gone, like the afterglow of sunset at the margin of starry silence."

— Rabindranath Tagore, Stray Birds

Section 3
A New Phase of My Life Journey

"The need of change arises only when you understand that there is something wrong going on in the present and you have to stand your ground, trusting your honesty."

The National Patrika Subscription Agencies

Following my graduation from Delhi University in September 1961, I had a span of approximately three months where I was not employed. During this period, I visited relatives in various cities, including Aligarh, Agra and Delhi. My efforts to secure a job involved applying to numerous small private companies and Government advertisements in the newspapers through advertised vacancies, but until December 1961, none of these attempts resulted in a job offer. However, in December 1961, I landed a role as a salesman at "The National Patrika Subscription Agencies", an agency representing publications from "SOVIET LAND" and other socialist countries.

Under the guidance of my boss, Mr. Pravin Rawat, the Sales Manager, I embarked on a tour across Madhya Pradesh and Rajasthan, encompassing cities like Bhopal, Ratlam, Indore, Mao, Dewas, Ujjain and eventually Kota.

During this tour, Mr. Rawat acquired a railway ticket cum pass for the entire month in the states of Madhya Pradesh and Rajasthan. This pass allowed us unrestricted travel on any train within these states and as a result, we predominantly travelled in unreserved compartments, foregoing reservations to accommodate our expedited travel itinerary. From Mr. Rawat, I gained invaluable insights into travelling, networking and establishing connections. Our approach was to present our magazines to anyone who showed interest and persuade them to subscribe.

The subscription charges were minimal and my proficiency in both English and Hindi was beneficial in convincing people to subscribe, especially for the English and Local language Soviet publications. My manager commended my sales skills and persuasive abilities.

Over the course of an extensive three-week tour, we primarily lodged in Dharmshala or Waiting/ Retiring Rooms at railway stations, utilising these facilities based on the privileges accorded by our pass. After returning from the tour, I resumed my role as a salesman at The National Patrika's stall in Connaught Place, New Delhi. Following a brief tenure there, I independently revisited the same areas in Madhya Pradesh and Rajasthan, reconnecting with those who had previously shown interest. We provided them with a set of Soviet literature, including calendars and magazines, for a trial period. While many individuals subscribed upon subsequent visits, approximately 20% were not persuaded, prompting us to discontinue visiting them.

Central Research Institute, Kasauli

Around this juncture, I, along with the aforementioned friends, received employment letters from the Central Research Institute, Kasauli. We were required to report to the institute within 15 days of receiving the appointment letter. Given the prospects of a Government job, I decided to resign from The National Patrika Subscription Agencies. My tenure at the agency spanned from January 1st, 1962 to July 2nd, 1962.

Meeting yet another Mentor - Shri Pukhraj Jain

An intriguing incident unfolded during my first visit to Kota alongside my manager. At the Aerodrome Circle, there stood a massive building housing about 10-12 shops and offices on the ground floor. The front side of this structure faced the circle, while its rear side was the residence of Shri Pukhraj Jain, a well-known transporter in the area. Mr. Jain showed a great deal of interest in me and the Soviet literature which we were promoting. On my second visit to his place, Mr. Jain warmly welcomed me into his sitting room and office, inviting me for a Marwari Pure Vegetarian Lunch, complete with generous servings of Desi Ghee.

After our meal, I politely asked Mr. Jain to subscribe to our publications for at least a year, explaining that it would greatly assist me. To my surprise, he pledged to subscribe not for one, but for three years. At the end of our meeting, he inquired about my satisfaction, to which I expressed my gratitude repeatedly. When he learned, I was planning to spend the night in the waiting room or retiring room at the Kota Railway Station, I asked him if he could introduce me to the tenants in all the shops within his building. He agreed but requested my patience.

During our conversation, Mr. Jain shared a painful and sad family story with me. He mentioned having four daughters and a son; three of his daughters were married and his youngest daughter and son were pursuing their studies. He revealed that one of his married daughters suffered from epilepsy and during one of her attacks, she would utter words that were incomprehensible to everyone except one of his other daughters, who could interpret her language and actions. Mr. Jain believed that during his first visit, all his daughters came together and during that time, the daughter suffering from epilepsy, had an attack. The other daughter claimed that the spirit of their late grandfather had entered her, telling them that the young boy who had previously visited was their son in the previous birth. This revelation made his family very affectionate and amiable towards me.

As our conversation continued, Mr. Jain inquired about my family background and education. When he discovered that I was passionate about my studies, had completed my B.Sc. and was a refugee from Pakistan facing financial constraints, he sympathised with my situation. He asked why I wasn't continuing my studies and I explained that my father's income was limited and that I needed to support my family. However, Mr. Jain insisted that I enroll in M.Sc., assuring me of financial support. I gratefully accepted his offer and promised to reach out for his help in the future.

Before parting ways, Mr. Jain insisted that I retrieve my belongings from the station and stay with him in his office-cum-house. I spent the night at his place and the next morning met all his tenants and other shops and offices near his building. Then I resumed my sales tour to Ratlam.

Job with Central Research Institute, Kasauli

My time at The Central Research Institute marked my second employment opportunity, a pivotal role as a Technical Supervisor in the Biological Standardisation and Quality Control Centre as well as the National Salmonella Department. Under the guidance of Dr. S.C. Agarwal, a distinguished individual with an M.D. and Ph.D. from London, I was exposed to a wealth of knowledge and an environment that emphasised discipline, leadership and exceptional character. This tenure enabled me to deepen my knowledge of bacteriological techniques, including the preparation of media, sterilisation processes and the sub-culturing of organisms, which significantly enhanced my professional skills.

With three other students from different departments, we made the collective decision to share accommodation, renting a spacious four-bedroom bungalow located approximately 1 km away from the institute. Additionally, we had two servant quarters, situated around 100 yards away from the main bungalow, on the hilly terrain. This property, originally owned by an English family, had changed hands and was currently under the ownership of a hotelier who operated a well-frequented restaurant near the institute, attracting several officers and workers.

A practice of the company that caught my attention

Our monthly salary amounted to Rs. 263/-. Despite allocating Rs. 125/- per month for the bungalow rent, we were able to manage the kitchen expenses & other miscellaneous within Rs. 130/- month. Meals were mainly taken at a nearby hotel, encompassing breakfast, lunch and dinner. Despite these expenditures, we managed to sustain small savings. Our work schedule from Monday to Saturday was from 9 A.M. to 5 P.M., incorporating an hour for lunch. However, we noticed a prevailing practice among everyone to sign the attendance register at 9 A.M., regardless of their actual arrival time. Following this norm, we, too, adhered to signing in at 9 A.M.

Initially, our experience at the institute was positive. Our work, the accommodation and the overall ambience in Kasauli were satisfactory. As part of a protocol within Government Departments during the 1960s, we were obligated to attend Hindi classes sponsored by the Government. Despite our prior knowledge of Hindi from University education, we attended these sessions. Our Hindi teacher, a young lady from Delhi University, gradually developed a rapport with us. However, after a few months, she shared her concerns about the Director of the institute, Mr. J.B. Shirvastav, citing inappropriate behaviour and dubious intentions, which deeply disturbed us as he was of the same age as the teacher's father.

We Decided to Raise Our Voices Against the Injustice

We confided in Mr. P.N. Sadhu, the Administrative Officer (A.O.), a Kashmiri gentleman, on deputation from the Ministry of Health in New Delhi. Mr. Sadhu had previously worked under my brother-in-law, Mr. Amar Nath Verma, who held the position of Under Secretary in the

Ministry of Health. Mr. Sadhu often extended his hospitality, inviting us for meals or tea at his house. We shared the troubling situation of the Hindi teacher's harassment by the Director with Mr. Sadhu and somehow, this information reached the Director's ears. This led us to speculate how the Director got wind of our conversation with Mr. Sadhu. Two prevailing theories emerged: one without being direct, Mr. Sadhu might have divulged our discussion to please the Director and the other suggesting that he might have disclosed our habitual late arrivals despite signing in at 9 A.M. However, the Director only took action against four of us by suspending us despite the fact that majority of employees were arriving late and signing in promptly. This suspension seemed unjust, lacking any prior notice or discussion.

In Kasauli, a small town devoid of courts or legal professionals, we sought legal counsel from a lawyer in Solan to challenge the Director's suspension. We managed to secure a stay order against the Director's decision. This turn of events deeply upset the Director, causing him significant shock and embarrassment. We later became aware of his extensive influence and powerful connections within the institute, the state and even at the National level.

The Matter was further taken to the Higher Authorities in Power

The Director of the Central Research Institute, Mr. Shrivastav, shared a close friendship with Chief Minister Sardar Pratap Singh Kairon of Punjab State. Sardar Kairon was a key figure aligned with the late Prime Minister, Mrs. Indira Gandhi. During that period, Punjab was a challenging state to govern and Sardar Kairon and his sons wielded substantial influence over the local populace, particularly the Sikhs. Notably, Sardar Kairon played a pivotal role in decisively quelling the Khalistani Movement with a firm hand. Indira Gandhi leaned on him and Mr. Shrivastav, with his connections, carried a significant influence that seemed akin to a Don-like figure. Mr. Shrivastav reached out to Mr. Verma in the Health Ministry in Delhi, briefing him on the entire episode. He expressed his reluctance to take back the suspension order, preferring not to engage in a dispute with young individuals of our age. Instead, he requested Mr. Verma to persuade his brother-in-law and his friends to resign from the job and assured that he would facilitate alternative, potentially better, employment either in Chandigarh, Punjab, or Delhi.

Upon discussing this with my family, I was told that Director of the Institute has offered jobs for two of my colleagues in Chandigarh and surrounding area. Mr. Hari Bijlani has made request to the Director for suitable job in Delhi. My family was swayed by the assurance of the Director, who later rose to become the Director General of Health and Family Welfare stationed in New Delhi. Upon my return to Kasauli, I relayed the conversations from Delhi to my colleagues and all of them agreed to the proposal set forth by Mr. Verma. Also Mr. Verma had influenced Administrative Officer Mr. Sadhu to persuade us to resign and seek new jobs that would offer better prospects in more developed areas instead of Kasauli, which is a backward area. He stressed the severity of the harsh winter conditions and strongly advised us to consider the Director's proposal. Mr. Verma assured us of the Director's credibility, emphasising his commitment to fulfilling promises, particularly due to the necessity of securing funding from the Ministry to sustain the Institute's operations.

Hari Bijlani secured a job in Delhi with the Construction Corporation of India, Vinod Sood landed a position in Delhi with the Fertiliser Corporation of India and another colleague got a job in Chandigarh. However, I refused the Director's offer, feeling deeply disturbed by the situation. This experience made me feel inadequate and powerless. My colleague Davender and I pondered over the Director's authority and inappropriate conduct. The Director held an M.Sc. in Biochemistry, while we had B.Sc. degrees in Chemistry, merely one step below his qualification.

Education Plays Pivotal Role in Getting Power and Position

Dr. Agarwal, my immediate supervisor in the institute, possessed a Ph.D., a step higher than the Director. We deliberated and concluded that our best course of action would either be to pursue further studies up to M.Sc. or consider migrating to the UK. However, financial constraints were a crucial factor in our decision-making process. After carefully considering my options, I decided to seek support from Shri Pukhraj Jain in Kota to further my studies. In a detailed discussion with Jain Sahib, he generously agreed to sponsor my M.Sc. studies. In return, I assured him that once I secured employment, I would repay the entire amount.

Upon my return to Delhi, I began the application process for M.Sc. in Microbiology/ Biochemistry. Microbiology was a relatively new subject in Indian Universities in 1962, with Maharaja Sayaji Rao University (M.S. University), Baroda and Punjab University offering the programme. Initially pleased with the admission offer from M.S. University, I sought advice from my professors. They suggested that pursuing a degree in the UK might offer better prospects due to the abundance of job opportunities. Acting on their advice, I applied for a work permit from the British Embassy, submitting attested copies of my academic and character certificates. Within six weeks, I received the work permit, opening doors to securing a job in the UK aligned with my qualifications.

Returning to Kota, I discussed both options with Mr. Jain, who sought opinions from his tenants. They overwhelmingly favoured migrating to the UK, emphasising the potential for substantial earnings and opportunities to bring over family members. Taking their advice to heart, I sought Mr. Jain's approval to fund my airfare, requesting Rs. 3000/- to cover the ticket cost and additional expenses.

After thorough discussions with my family, Mr. Amar Nath Verma, friends and professors from Delhi University, the consensus leaned towards relocating to the UK under the work permit scheme. This decision was seen as a means to improve our family's financial situation and support the education and marriage of younger siblings and elder sisters. In a profound conversation with Mr. Gupta, it was unanimously agreed that I should migrate to the UK, secure a job and save money to facilitate my brother's relocation later on.

Recognising the need to counteract the misuse of power and authority witnessed in Kasauli, I resolved to attain better qualifications than Mr. J.B. Shrivastav to wield influence responsibly. Thus, by the end of March 1963, I made the conclusive decision to migrate to the UK and informed Mr. Jain about my resolution, requesting financial support for my airfare expenses.

My last day of employment with the Central Research Institute in Kasauli was on February 28th, 1963.

Summary

Section 3: A New Phase of My Life Journey

Major incidents:

1. Joining "The National Patrika Subscription."
2. Job offer from Central Research Institute, Kasauli.
3. Joining "Central Research Institute, Kasauli".
4. Meeting Shri Pukhraj Jain at Kota.

Learning:

1. Incidences in life teach more than the lessons of textbooks
2. Sometimes, the encounter with a complete stranger can change the entire course of one's life journey and the perspective to look at life.

Chapter defining quote:

"A deeper sense of humility and respect comes after encountering an experience one never want to go through again in one's life"

Section 4

Employment After Graduation

"Destiny impacts our lives in the most unexpected ways."

Part 1: The First Job Always Remains Close to Heart

Upon my return to Delhi in early March 1963, my father informed me about a recent arrival from England named Sardar Arjun Singh Sually. He was temporarily lodging at the residence of a laundry shop owner across the street from my father's store. Intrigued by the prospects in the UK, my father suggested I visit the shop to discuss securing a work permit and exploring job opportunities there. Through multiple conversations with Arjun Singh Ji, I learned about his unconventional background. He lacked formal education and had previously earned a living by predicting fortunes using cards on street corners in India.

In England, he had shifted to selling gift items to sailors at the dockyard where he resided with his family. He had a return ticket booked for London on June 29, 1963 and proposed that I accompany him to his home in Swansea, South Wales, where he assured me of employment opportunities. My family found comfort in the idea of me travelling with an Indian already settled in the UK, potentially offering accommodation. After deliberations within the family, we decided to journey with Arjun Singh Ji to the UK. However, obtaining a passport became an urgent need. Fortunately, I had a friend, Mr. Bhisham Kohli, who held a managerial position at Eros Cinema in Jangpura, New Delhi. Leveraging Mr. Kohli's connections in the passport office, I managed to expedite the process and obtained my passport within just 1 ½ months. Sardar Arjun Singh Ji was impressed by the swift issuance of my passport, especially considering his own prolonged struggle to secure one. With the passport in hand, I reached out to Mr. Pukhraj Jain in Kota for assistance in purchasing an air ticket from Air India. Mr. Jain promptly arranged to send the required sum of Rs. 3000/-. In adherence to the regulations of the time, which allowed travellers to carry a maximum of 3 Pounds, I acquired the permitted amount from the Jeena Travel Agency in Connaught Place, New Delhi. With all necessary travel documents— passport, work permit, visa and the permitted 3 pounds—I booked an economy class air ticket from Delhi to London via Air India.

Role of Mr. Arjun Singh Ji in my Life

Arjun Singh Ji assured me that there would be no issues and that I could travel with him to the UK. On June 29, 1963, at the age of less than 22 years, Arjun Singh Ji and I boarded an Air India flight from Delhi bound for London. Airline services during that era, including Air India, were exceptional, offering extensive meal options and beverages. However, once airborne, Arjun Singh Ji started consuming alcoholic drinks excessively, eventually losing control and becoming heavily intoxicated. This was a disconcerting experience for me, as I had never witnessed someone in such a state before.

Sensing my discomfort, he confided in me, sharing his grievances about his brother's deceitful actions, including an undisclosed marriage. Expressing his frustration, he spent our remaining funds on phone calls to family and friends, lamenting about his brother's behaviour and betrayal. As a result, we were left with no money except for the bus fare from the airport to the railway station, as the 3 pounds he had taken from me was spent on purchasing whisky from the plane's duty-free shop.

Stranded in London without enough money for train tickets to Swansea, Arjun Singh Ji sought assistance from the Station master. Thankfully, the Station master facilitated our ticket purchase, with Arjun Singh Ji promising to repay the amount upon our arrival at the Swansea railway station. Upon reaching Swansea, we were greeted by someone in a Mini Morris car, akin to a Maruti 800 and we arrived at Arjun Singh's residence around 11 P.M. I was assigned a small room with a single bed, but that night, sleep eluded me due to the heated arguments that erupted among them.

Learning and Unlearning about Perspectives

The following morning brought a semblance of normalcy as we gathered for tea. The house regained its calm atmosphere, leading me to believe that Arjun Singh's earlier behaviour was influenced by alcohol. He introduced me to his wife and two daughters, aged 17 and 10 years, both well-behaved. His wife was kind and

Singh appeared sober in the morning. Later, I learned from his relatives and friends that after consuming alcohol, Arjun Singh Ji often lost control of himself, unaware of his behaviour. I spent about 4 to 5 days resting at their house before joining him in his business activities.

Arjun Singh Ji took charge of a business previously managed by his younger brother during his absence, involving the sale of gift items to sailors in ships and dock areas. He mentioned that his brother had entrusted the business to him until his return. I closely observed his marketing methods, which included packing items into a sizeable suitcase and transporting them on the back of a bicycle to the ships docked at the dockyard. Once aboard, he displayed the items on tables for sailors from various countries to peruse and make selections.

Negotiations on prices followed, often resulting in cash payments or exchanges for liquor such as whisky, brandy, cigarettes and cigars. We typically visited 2 to 3 ships daily, spending about 1 to 2 hours on each. Despite his success, Singh believed this trade wasn't suitable for me and instead encouraged me to register at the employment exchange and explore job opportunities in companies he personally recommended.

A Job at the Chemical Factory

After several unsuccessful attempts to secure employment, I finally found a job at a Chemical factory specialising in the production of plastic flexible tubes of different diameters. My role involved working on the assembly line alongside my colleagues. The factory operated in three shifts—morning, evening and night—with payments calculated hourly based on the specific shift. Overtime rates varied, with the morning shift paying a standard amount, the afternoon shift offering one and a half time and the night shift providing double pay. The working schedule typically involved rotating through one week each of morning, afternoon and night shifts.

The work at the tube manufacturing factory was undoubtedly demanding, requiring both physical and mental exertion. Despite the challenges, it proved financially rewarding, motivating me to eagerly take on extra shifts, particularly during the afternoon shift and expressing my readiness to work overtime whenever necessary. Fortunately, my considerate supervisor often granted me additional shifts, mixing morning and afternoon shifts, afternoon and night shifts, or night and morning shifts. This not only allowed me to earn more but also enabled me to accumulate significant earnings within a short period. With my income steadily increasing, I decided to rent a room in Mr. Singh's house, paying a nominal fee of 4 pounds per week for accommodation. Additionally, I contributed about 3 pounds per week for boarding, resulting in a total weekly expense of around 7 pounds. Transportation costs were minimal, especially during the night shift, as the company provided taxis and meals, making the night shift financially advantageous and appealing due to the additional perks. By the end of 1963, I had diligently saved enough money to repay the Rs. 3000/- borrowed from Shri Pukhraj Jain of Kota. Without delay, I promptly sent the repayment from Swansea through Lloyd Bank.

By April of the following year, I was financially prepared to cover the airfare for my elder brother, Shri Sudarshan Kumar Shingari, whose arrival in June 1964 necessitated adjustments in our living expenses, including increased rent and food expenses.

My dedication and commitment to work were recognised by my supervisor, who appreciated my punctuality, consistent attendance and willingness to take on extra work during overtime. I took the initiative to inquire about job opportunities for my brother, leading to his employment at the same company in July 1964. Both of us continued our employment there until April 1965.

Unfortunately, a regrettable incident occurred during our stay at Mr. Singh's residence during a late night, escalating into a heated argument between us. In the aftermath, we decided to vacate the room and relocate with the help of a colleague, Mohammad Ali, to a nearby house.

A New Beginning at the Cardiff, South Wales

Later, in April, we made the decision to move to Newport, a town in close proximity to Cardiff, South Wales, attracted by its employment opportunities in the steel and transportation sectors. Our new landlord, Yusuf Khan, a Pakistani provided us with a room in his house, where we settled temporarily until I secured admission in any college around Cardiff / Newport.

I commenced my search for suitable college offering Engineering courses, considering their programme structures and tuition fees.

Eventually, I found the Glamorgan College of Technology at Llantwit Road, Treforest, Pontypridd, which offered Chemical Engineering. Dr. D.P. Evans, the principal, generously spent time understanding my academic background, challenges and aspirations. He recommended that I complete the admission application for the four-year sandwich degree course in Chemical Engineering, which involved alternating between six months in college, five months in industries and a one-month break. This structure perfectly aligned with my goal of simultaneous learning and earning, prompting my decision to join the college if granted admission.

Joined Glamorgan College of Technology

In late May, I revisited the college to complete the application form and met with the Principal. After reviewing my application, which included certificates from Delhi University and work experience documents from the Central Serum Research Institute, he offered me admission to the first year of a four-year course. Due to my prior B.Sc. in pure sciences from Delhi University, I appealed for exemption from the first year's curriculum, as I had already covered similar subjects.

I requested admission directly into the second-year. However, the Principal initially hesitated to grant my request and consulted with the Head of the Chemical Engineering Department to discuss my plea for exemption. The department head cited a previous case of a student admitted with a B.Sc. degree from Bombay who struggled in the second-year due to insufficient foundational knowledge. Consequently, I enrolled in the first year of the four-year sandwich course.

My Poor Performance in the First Year Was a Blessing in Disguise

In July 1965, I commenced my studies in the first year of the four-year degree programme. The college provided me with hostel accommodation on campus, which was incredibly convenient, saving both time and money on commuting. However, after three months, my performance in the first term exam was unsatisfactory. Dr. Evans, the college Principal, summoned me to his office to discuss my results. When questioned about my poor performance, I found myself unable to articulate a response. Recognising my struggle to communicate, Dr. Evans inquired whether I faced challenges understanding lectures in English, to which I nodded in agreement. In response, he promptly instructed the Registrar and Secretary to arrange for me to lodge as a paying guest (digs) with a landlady residing near the college. They assured me that staying with this family would not only help me with English but also accustom me to the Welsh dialect.

A New Dawn for me in the Pursuit of Learning: Mrs. Lewis and her rules!

The college facilitated my accommodation with Mrs. Lewis, located very close to the college gate, charging 4 pounds per week for the digs. Before transitioning from the hostel to Mrs. Lewis's residence, she introduced me to her husband, Mr. Lewis, a coal miner. They were a middle-aged couple living alone without children.

Mrs. Lewis outlined some crucial rules:

1. Mr. Lewis was strict and maintained discipline and I was expected to adhere to these standards without compromise.
2. No visitors were allowed in the house.
3. I needed to return home by 7 P.M., or I would have to spend the night outside.
4. I wouldn't be given a main door key.

5. Timeliness was critical for breakfast and dinner; lateness would result in my plate
6. I had to eat what was served or go hungry.
7. No lunch during week days and only on Sunday.
8. No alcoholic drinks were permitted inside the house.

Upon moving into Mrs. Lewis's house, she assigned me a small room and introduced me to the three other students residing there—one from Pakistan and the remaining two were English. She provided the meal timings for breakfast, dinner and Sunday lunch, along with the arrangement for a hot water bath, allowed once a week, with fixed time and quantity due to fuel scarcity. Heating was limited to a coal fire in the drawing room, sourced from Mr. Lewis's mine where he worked. Living with an English family enhanced my grasp of the language and its accent.

Mrs. Lewis displayed a kind and compassionate nature. During a particularly harsh winter, my Indian clothing proved inadequate for the cold. Mrs. Lewis noticed and aware of my financial constraints, bought me an overcoat from a "jumble sale." Though second-hand, the clothes were nearly new and I felt grateful and content to use them. Over time, Mrs. Lewis grew friendly and treated me akin to her own son, despite her strict, disciplined attitude and behaviour. She maintained fixed quantities for breakfast and dinner and declined second helpings if requested.

A funny encounter at the dining table

One of the fellow students staying with us was a Pakistani Muslim named Syed Umar Qadri, who abstained from pork consumption, akin to Hindus refraining from beef. I informed the landlady and her husband about our dietary preferences to avoid any servings of cow or pork meat. Syed Umar and I became good friends. Observing his smaller food portions, I occasionally manoeuvred a planned statement by suggesting his meat was from a pig (Khanjir).

He'd promptly ask me to remove it, saying "Hata hata" (implying to take it away from his plate). Swiftly, I'd shift the meat to my plate before the landlady noticed, ensuring I got extra meat, primarily lamb (void of cow or pork). Once again, I emphasise the wonderful relationship I fostered with Mrs. and Mr. Lewis—I was content living there. After the term ended, my performance in the final exam after three months was Outstanding.

Recognition for my Efforts and Sincerity

The college Principal and the Head of the Department expressed satisfaction, leading me to receive the FIRST PRIZE awarded by The Imperial Smelting Corporation Ltd. for outstanding work in the College Associateship in Chemical Engineering. A copy of the certificate is attached in the Awards and Scholarships Section.

Before beginning the second-year curriculum, I underwent a five-month training programme at the "Wales Gas Board" office in Cardiff, under the guidance of Mr. Farmer, the training officer. This comprehensive training covered various office sections such as the drawing office, marketing, billing and complaints.

During this period, I received a salary of 15 pounds per week. Following the completion of this training, I returned to college to pursue the second-year course, maintaining a commendable performance that led to my promotion to the third-year. Upon finishing the second-year, I embarked on a training stint at Fisons Fertilisers Limited in Avon mouth, England, from May 1st to September 22nd 1966.

Subsequently, my third-year training took place at British Hydrocarbon Chemicals Limited.

Throughout these training periods, I gained valuable practical experience and honed my skills, preparing me for the challenges ahead in my career.

Upon successfully completing my training at Wales Gas Board, Fisons Fertilisers Limited and British Hydrocarbon Chemicals Limited, coupled with my exceptional performance throughout the four-year course, I was awarded Second Class Honours (1st Division) for my Academic achievements and Industrial training.

My Academic Recognition

The Council for National Academic Awards granted me the degree of BACHELOR OF SCIENCE (B.Sc.) in Chemical Engineering, effective from July 5th , 1968. This recognition was a testament to my dedication, hard work and the quality of education and training I received at GLAMORGAN COLLEGE OF TECHNOLOGY, as well as my commitment to excellence in both academic and practical aspects of my field.

Joined University Of Wales for M.Sc. Chem. Eng. and Ph.D. in Chemical Engineering

After attaining my B.Sc. Hons. (1st Class), I pursued admission to the M.Sc. course at the University College of Swansea, University of Wales. In a letter dated April 9, 1968, the Assistant Registrar notified me of my acceptance into the Chemical Engineering Department, with the course set to commence in October 1968. This offer hinged upon achieving at least a 2nd Class Division Hons. Degree in my previous B.Sc. course.

I successfully completed my M.Sc. in Chemical Engineering, confirmed by the Academic Secretary on March 19, 1970. Following this, I endeavoured to secure a Research studentship sponsored by the "Welsh Plate and Sheet Manufacturers Association," competing with other M.Sc. graduates for various opportunities. However, despite my efforts, I did not secure the aforementioned Research studentship, as conveyed in a letter from Dr. J.C. Lee dated July 31, 1968, from the University of Wales' Department of Chemical Engineering.

On October 1, 1969, I received a letter from the Registrar, confirming a Research studentship in the Chemical Engineering Department worth £530 plus fees, recommended by the Head of Department, Prof. Richardson. Subsequent communications on March 19, 1970 and April 27, 1970, indicated the successful completion of my M.Sc. degree and an increase in my Research studentship to £880 per annum plus fees from March 1, 1970, to September 30, 1970. This grant was extended for another year from October 1, 1970, as per a letter dated August 19, 1970 and further prolonged until September 30, 1972, according to a letter dated July 20, 1971.

Prof. Richardson also recommended me as a Student Demonstration/Tutorial Assistant in the Department of Chemical Engineering for 1970-71 session, compensated with remuneration at £15 per hour for a total of £60 for 4 hours. Throughout my M.Sc. and Ph.D. courses, I received consistent financial support. Although my grant was valid until September 1972, I completed my Ph.D. thesis ahead of schedule, returning to India in March after wrapping up my work by February 1972.

Upon my return, I updated my supervisor, Dr. John Conder, on the examination's outcome and implemented the Examiner's recommendations. Dr. Conder assured me that my stipend would continue until September and requested my presence in October to finalise my project and hand over university belongings. Additionally, I was informed that I could collect my Ph.D. degree during the convocation in late 1972 or opt for receiving it in absentia.

My academic journey, from my B.Sc. to M.Sc. and Ph.D., was generously funded by scholarships and Research grants from British Industries, notably sponsored by Bush Bosh and Allen.

Interestingly, I did not transfer funds from India to the UK; instead, I sent money back home, saving a significant amount from the grant to kick start my entrepreneurial venture in India. This saved sum, along with additional savings from my Research grant, served as the Initial Capital for my New project.

Planning my Entrepreneurial Journey during my Ph.D.

During my Ph.D. tenure, I harboured a strong determination to establish a small company in India specialising in manufacturing Gas Chromatographs and other instruments not readily available domestically. These products were typically imported from countries like the UK, USA and Japan. With this vision in mind, I conceptualised a laboratory Gas Chromatograph equipped with two detectors: Thermal Conductivity (TCD) and Flame Ionisation

Detectors (FID). Once I finalised the design, I engaged in discussions with the Head and Technical Staff of the Electronics Department, individuals knowledgeable in servicing similar types of equipments used in our department.

To initiate this plan, I acquired two Gas Chromatographs (GC)—one with a Thermal Conductivity Detector (TCD) and another with a Flame Ionisation Detector (FID) along with an isothermal oven—from Jones Chromatography Limited (JCL). The Managing Director of JCL frequently visited our department and due to my preference for their equipment, we developed a cordial relationship. My strategy was to engage with a newer product from a smaller company, discussing the design under the pretext of developing an industrial-scale GC using a similar separation technique.

This approach proved fruitful and Mr. Jones extended considerable assistance. Our objective was to use these laboratory models alongside my production scale prototype GC to analyse the composition of separated components within the mixture at various stages.

As we collaborated closely with Jones Chromatography, it became evident that they didn't suspect any ill intentions or attempts to copy their GC design. Instead, we made substantial modifications to their equipment and finalised our own design, adhering to JCL specifications. Several modifications were made in mechanical design and circuitry, improving stability, noise level and reliability, which were appreciated by Mr. Colin Jones, Managing Director and Mr. Paul Cravous of Jones Chromatography Limited.

I managed to save a significant portion of my grant, providing sufficient funds to purchase the components and sub-assemblies required to create two prototype GCs. To ensure the viability of my plan, I discussed it with Dr. John Conder, who then joined me in meeting the Head of Department, Prof. Richardson, seeking his perspectives and approval. Prof. Richardson was pleased to learn about my intention to contribute my expertise to India's advancement and granted permission to construct two units within the department using my materials, permitting me to transport them to India.

Successfully constructing and thoroughly testing two prototype GC systems, I meticulously compiled a complete component list with specifications and relevant details, facilitating procurement in India. The project was meticulously documented and the units were carefully packed within the department, ready for shipping to India along with my personal belongings when I returned in February/March 1972.

During the testing phase, I engaged Mr. Shrish Bhailal Patel from the Electrical Engineering Department, offering him a 50% partnership in the venture, to which he eagerly agreed. Mr. Patel's keen interest in returning to India post-education and his background made him a suitable partner. This collaborative effort paved the way for our venture's success. Photographs were taken with Professor Richardson, the Head of the Department of Chemical Engineering, along with Mr. Ron Beed, the Mechanical Workshop In-charge and Mr. Davis, the Electronics Laboratory In-charge. Without obtaining the Head's permission and without full cooperation from Mr. Ron Beed and Mr. Davis, it was not possible to complete the project before the deadline. Their support was crucial, as it allowed us to save almost a year on the project timeline, for which we received payment.

The money saved from this project became the Seed Capital for the establishment of CIC.

Without the timely completion of this project and the financial benefit it provided, the inception of CIC would have been significantly delayed or may not have been possible at all. Therefore, the cooperation and assistance from individuals like Mr. Ron Beed and Mr. Davis played a pivotal role in the founding of our company and its subsequent success.

Photo with Professor Richardson

Notably, my extensive educational journey, spanning from B.Sc. to Ph.D., attracted numerous job offers from Educational institutions and the Chemical Industry, underscoring the value placed on higher education in various professional sectors.

Photo with Mr. Davis

Sub-Assemblies of my Ph.D. Project – Production of Gas Chromatograph

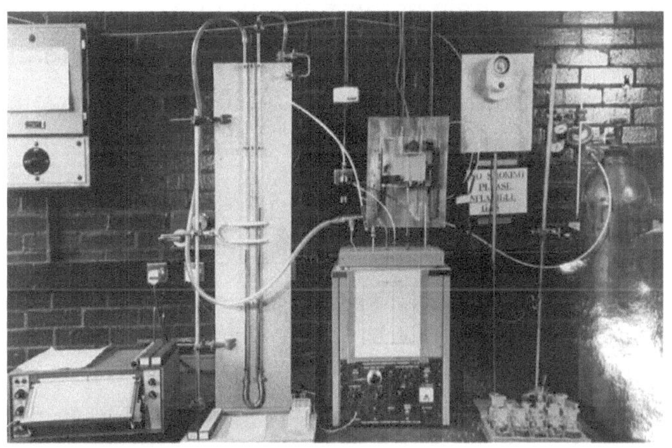

Part II: Importance of Education

A Catalyst for Character Building, Career Advancement and Self + National Progress

Education plays a pivotal and indispensable role in the life of every individual, in our societal fabric and fundamentally in the overall development and progress of a nation. It serves as the cornerstone upon which societies are built and civilisations thrive. In today's world, education has evolved into a highly sophisticated and advanced system, with individuals taking immense pride in their academic achievements and professional designations. However, despite the strides made in education, the persistent challenges and issues plaguing our society remain largely unabated.

The contemporary educational paradigm primarily focuses on academic prowess, often equating success with the acquisition of degrees and certificates. While this emphasis on intellectual development is crucial, it alone does not suffice to address the multifaceted challenges faced by the society. The prevailing education system, which prioritises rote *("ratta")* learning, material possessions and personal achievements, falls short in addressing the deep-rooted issues such as poverty, inequality, hypocrisy and corruption that continue to afflict our communities.

It is imperative, therefore, to reevaluate and reformulate the objectives of education to align more closely with the alleviation of societal woes and the cultivation of moral values and ethical principles. As Swami Vivekananda, the revered Indian Hindu monk, philosopher and spiritual leader rightly articulated, *"True education should not merely focus on intellectual pursuits but should also instil compassion, integrity and a sense of social responsibility."* By nurturing individuals who are not only academically proficient but also empathetic and altruistic, education can serve as a catalyst for positive social change and contribute significantly to the betterment of society as a whole.

"Education is the manifestation of the perfection already in the man."

"Education is the panacea for the evils in the world."

However, it is essential to underscore that education must be tailored to suit the specific needs and cultural context of each society. There is no one-size-fits-all approach to education, as different societies possess unique values, traditions and challenges. The right type of education for a particular society is one that is sensitive to its cultural heritage, socio-economic dynamics and aspirations.

In the Indian context, the significance of education cannot be overstated, as it serves as the cornerstone of societal progress and individual empowerment. Education in India plays a multifaceted role, encompassing not only academic learning but also the cultivation of essential virtues and life skills. It is through education that individuals acquire the necessary qualities to navigate life with integrity, humility and moral uprightness. Moreover, education equips individuals with job-oriented skills, empowering them to contribute meaningfully to the economy and society.

The ideal education system in India should aim to integrate these essential qualities into the fabric of society, fostering a culture of truthfulness, politeness, honesty and humility. By instilling these virtues in the younger generation, education can serve as a catalyst for positive social change and Nation's development. Furthermore, education should extend beyond the individual, contributing to the overall betterment of families, communities and the nation as a whole.

Some of the critical requirements and outcomes of an effective education system include promoting inclusive learning environments that cater to the diverse needs of students, fostering critical thinking and problem-solving skills and encouraging lifelong learning and personal growth. Additionally, education should strive to bridge the gap between theoretical knowledge and practical application, preparing students for real-world challenges and opportunities. Ultimately, the true measure of the success of an education system lies in its ability to empower individuals to lead fulfilling lives and contribute meaningfully to society.

Character Building

Education serves as a potent instrument for shaping the character and moral compass of individuals, instilling in them values, ethics and a profound sense of responsibility. In the context of Indian society, characterised by its rich cultural tapestry and diverse heritage, education serves as a vital bridge between tradition and modernity. Schools and colleges, beyond merely imparting academic knowledge, play a pivotal role in nurturing essential qualities such as discipline, empathy and respect for diversity among students.

Beyond the confines of textbooks and classrooms, education serves to mold individuals into conscientious and socially responsible citizens. By fostering a deep sense of civic duty and community engagement, education equips individuals with the tools to contribute meaningfully to the social fabric. Through exposure to literature, history and the arts, education not only cultivates intellectual curiosity but also nurtures a profound sense of cultural identity and heritage.

Moreover, education serves as a powerful catalyst for promoting tolerance, empathy and understanding among individuals from diverse backgrounds. By encouraging dialogue, critical thinking and open-mindedness, education fosters an environment where differences are celebrated rather than vilified. Through interactions with peers and exposure to various perspectives, students learn to appreciate the richness of human diversity and develop the empathy necessary for building inclusive and harmonious societies.

In essence, education in Indian society plays a multifaceted role beyond the mere transmission of knowledge. It serves as a transformative force, shaping individuals into compassionate, culturally aware and socially responsible citizens who are equipped to navigate the complexities of the modern world while upholding the values and traditions of their cultural heritage.

Job-oriented Skills

In the dynamic landscape of the global economy, education emerges as the cornerstone for acquiring the skills essential for building a successful and rewarding career. Particularly in India, where the youth population is burgeoning at a rapid pace, investing in education holds immense potential for driving socio-economic advancement. *Education empowers individuals with the technical acumen, analytical prowess and adaptive problem-solving abilities required to thrive in today's competitive job market. With the advent of specialised vocational training and tailored educational programmes, individuals can further augment their employability and skill sets, thereby enhancing their prospects for meaningful employment.* These specialised initiatives cater to the specific demands of various industries, equipping individuals with the practical skills and knowledge needed to excel in their chosen fields. By aligning education with industry requirements, vocational training ensures that individuals are well-prepared to navigate the complexities of the modern workplace and make tangible contributions to the economy.

Moreover, education serves as a powerful catalyst for personal growth and economic prosperity on a broader scale. By equipping individuals with the tools to pursue their aspirations and realise their potential, education empowers them to chart their own path towards success and fulfilment. As individuals acquire new knowledge and skills, they not only enhance their earning potential but also contribute to the overall productivity and competitiveness of the economy.

In essence, education plays a pivotal role in shaping the trajectory of individuals' lives and driving socio-economic progress. By fostering a culture of lifelong learning and skill development, education paves the way for personal empowerment, economic resilience and sustainable livelihoods in an increasingly dynamic and interconnected world.

Improvement in Family, Society and Nation

Education serves as a transformative force, catalysing positive change at both the micro and macro levels of society. At the micro level, within the confines of the family unit, education empowers individuals to make informed decisions that profoundly impact their well-being and that of their loved ones. *Educated individuals possess the knowledge and skills necessary to navigate various aspects of life, including health, financial management and family planning.* By leveraging their educational background, they can adopt healthier lifestyles, make sound financial choices and plan for the future, thereby contributing to the overall stability and prosperity of the household.

On a broader societal scale, education plays a pivotal role in fostering civic engagement and social cohesion. Educated citizens are more likely to actively participate in community initiatives, advocate for social justice and work towards the betterment of society as a whole. Through their involvement in volunteer activities, grassroots movements and advocacy efforts, educated individuals contribute to the creation of a more equitable and inclusive society, where the needs of all members are recognised and addressed.

At the National level, the importance of education cannot be overstated, as it serves as the cornerstone of sustainable development, innovation and global competitiveness. A well-educated populace forms the backbone of a thriving economy and a progressive society. By nurturing a skilled workforce, fostering creativity and critical thinking and promoting lifelong learning, education fuels innovation and drives economic growth. Moreover, an educated citizenry is better equipped to adapt to the demands of a rapidly evolving global landscape, positioning the nation for success in an increasingly interconnected world.

In summary, education acts as a powerful catalyst for positive transformation, empowering individuals, strengthening communities and driving National progress. By investing in education at all levels, societies can unlock human potential, foster inclusive development and build a brighter future for generations to come.

Overcoming Ignorance

Ignorance stands as a formidable barrier to progress, yet education serves as its antidote. Particularly in the Indian context, education empowers individuals to challenge outdated beliefs, question societal norms and actively contribute to the eradication of ignorance.

It cultivates a scientific mindset, fosters critical thinking skills and promotes a rational approach to problem-solving. By providing individuals with access to information and broadening their perspectives, education transforms them into agents of positive change within their communities. Overcoming ignorance is not merely an individual responsibility; it is a collective endeavour essential for the intellectual and moral advancement of the entire nation.

In summary, the significance of education in Indian society cannot be overstated. It forms the bedrock of character development, career advancement and societal progress. Education equips individuals with the tools to navigate the complexities of the modern world, enabling them to make meaningful contributions to their families, communities and the Nation at large. To fully realise the transformative potential of education, it is imperative for policymakers, educators and society as a whole to prioritise and invest in a comprehensive and inclusive educational system tailored to meet the diverse needs of the population. Only through such concerted efforts can India harness the power of education to build a brighter and more equitable future for all.

It remains an undeniable truth that today's youth are the future citizens of tomorrow. However, it is equally true that the quality of these future citizens depends heavily on the actions and guidance provided by today's elders and educators, as well as the type of education they receive. Therefore, the responsibility lies not only with the younger generation but also with the older generation and the educational institutions entrusted with shaping minds and character. By imparting quality education and instilling values that promote integrity, empathy and civic responsibility, we can ensure that the citizens of tomorrow are well-equipped to contribute positively to society and lead it towards progress and prosperity.

Summary

Section 4: Employment After Graduation

Major incidents:

1. Meeting Mr. Arjun Singh Sually. Landing in UK with new hopes.
2. First job outside India – still understanding the process of financial stability.
3. Joining Glamorgan College of Technology. Encounter with Mrs. Lewis and her strict rules.
4. Joining University of Wales for M.Sc. Chemical Engineering and Ph.D. in Chemical Engineering.
5. Beginning of my entrepreneurial journey on my own. Career Planning for Chromatography.

Learning:

1. The major learning come from the life experiences, both at personal and professional levels.

2. Adjustment might look weird at the beginning – but it's shaping up us, to become our best versions.
3. Consistency in efforts with honest intentions can lead one to achieve the desired outcome.

Chapter defining quote:

"Education is a progressive discovery of our ignorance."

Section 5

The Glorious Years - 1972 to 1975

"A true homecoming."

YEARS 1972-1975 HAPPENED TO BE THE GLORIOUS YEARS IN MY ENTIRE CAREER BECAUSE OF THE FOLLOWING:

- Started Instrumentation Company in Baroda, Gujarat in the Year 1972
- Participation in International Industrial Exhibition ASIA 1972 at Pragati Maidan, New Delhi.
- Marriage with Dr. Mrs. Kiran Shingari in 1972
- Manufacturing of GC in 1973
- Purchase of know-how for recorder from NCL, Pune in 1973
- Purchase of Land in GIDC, Baroda in 1973
- Construction of CIC Factory
- Purchase for know-how for ECD from BARC, Mumbai in 1975

I am very sure that all readers will agree with me that 1972-1975 were glorious years. This is narrated in this chapter.

Returning Home to my Motherland

After the completion of my Ph.D. journey and the successful submission of my thesis, which underwent corrections and acceptance following a personal interview at Cambridge University, I was given the green signal to return to India. Both my supervisors Dr. John Conder and the Head of the Department of Chemical Engineering were immensely pleased with the acceptance of my work. They acknowledged and appreciated that I had managed to save a year within the allocated project time frame. Prof. Richardson, recognising the significance of this achievement, permitted me to seek assistance from the workshop staff for packing my belongings, including two prototype Gas Chromatograph systems which I have built while doing my Ph.D. in the Chemical Engineering department in wooden boxes stored in the department's storage area. The workshop staff and my colleagues extended tremendous help in packing the items for shipment to India by sea.

My childhood friend, Mr. D.P. Gupta, working as a Chief Engineer at the Delhi Electrical Supply Undertaking (DESU), had made a request for a Philips colour television, the largest size available in England. As per his request, the TV was packed alongside my luggage for dispatch to India. Under the department's approval, the van was arranged to transfer my belongings to the shipping agent in Swansea.

After the shipment of all my luggage in wooden crates, I departed London on 7th March 1972 and arrived in New Delhi the following day. An incident of significance upon my arrival at Delhi Airport is worth narrating. My close friend, Bhisham Chand Kohli, who managed a liaison office and had strong political connections, met me at the airport. He took me directly from the immigration counter to his parked vehicle. Upon reaching home in Lajpat Nagar, as I unpacked my suitcase and bags, I offered Bhisham to choose anything he wished from the items I had brought from England.

During this process, Bhisham noticed a Webley Scott revolver in my belongings and was alarmed. He immediately informed me that we should have declared the firearm to customs and paid the necessary duties. Swiftly, we rushed back to the airport and declared the revolver at customs, paying the required customs duty. However, customs authorities informed us that the firearm could only be released upon submission of a valid firearm licence, which I did not possess. Bhisham assured me that he would arrange the necessary licence.

True to his word, within a week, Bhisham carefully organised the issuance of a legal and valid firearm licence from Delhi authorities. Once the licence was obtained, he accompanied me back to the airport customs, where we paid the storage fees and obtained the revolver.

Clearing of our luggage including Two Self-built GC and 1 TV from Bombay Custom Office located at the Dock Yard.

In Bombay, my maternal uncle, Mr. P.N. Anand, was holding the position of Director General of Shipping. He and his family were residing in the affluent area of Napian Sea Road. When I called my aunt to discuss clearing my luggage from Bombay Customs at the docks, she consulted with my uncle. He informed me that I had to personally come to Bombay to complete the necessary customs formalities and pay the duty for the new TV, as it wasn't permitted. He clarified that only used old TVs were allowed to be brought into the country if migrating from another nation to one's own. He advised that the process would take around 5-6 working days and there was a possibility of the TV being confiscated as it was a banned item. Consequently, I travelled to Bombay to stay at my aunt and uncle's house, but within five days, he had to leave for Delhi due to official work without resolving the customs matter.

The experience left me deeply disappointed as I had never encountered such issues during my nine-year stay in England. Additionally, I was taken aback by the attitude of my aunt and uncle. Upon my arrival in Bombay from Baroda via train, I took an auto to my aunt's residence on Napion Sea Road. However, upon learning that I had arrived in an auto, my aunt expressed dissatisfaction, insisting that I should only come to their house in a taxi. She remarked that arriving in an auto affected their reputation and status in the colony, which was home to many senior Government officers. This incident hurt me deeply and I decided not to visit their house in the future.

Around fifteen days later, I returned to Bombay. Upon reaching Bombay Central Railway Station at around 5 A.M., I freshened up at the waiting room and had breakfast at the station before heading to the dockyard. There, I inquired about the best clearing agent in the docks, following recommendations from people around the area. Subsequently, I reached the clearance agent's office at 9:30 A.M. and met the head Incharge of the office. Explaining my situation, I expressed my desire to have my luggage cleared by the evening. He assured me that it could be done but quoted charges of Rs. 5000 for his services, Rs. 1500 for miscellaneous expenses and the customs duty. I accepted his offer under the condition that the goods would be cleared and put on the train departing from Bombay Central to Baroda at 5 P.M. He agreed, stating I had to pay the TTE (Travelling Ticket Examiner) Rs. 200 and a sum to the coolie (porter). I accepted these terms.

He successfully cleared my luggage from customs and assigned a person to accompany me to the railway station. By 3:30 in the afternoon, we were at the platform awaiting the 4 P.M. train. The agent's representative managed the railway ticket, arranged with the TTE and the coolie and eventually placed the luggage in the train's brake van. The main items included a TV box, two boxes of Gas Chromatographs and a box of used goods, tools and parts. After securing the booking, I called my aunt at her Napion Sea Road residence to inform her of successfully clearing and boarding the train to Baroda. When she inquired about my visit, I explained that I arrived in the morning and was returning in the evening with my luggage after getting cleared from customs. I refrained from visiting her house, stating that I couldn't afford a taxi, considering my current standard was limited to travelling by auto and bus. I explained that I was financially constrained, unable to afford luxury when I hadn't yet earned a single rupee.

Mr. P.N. Anand had previously provided a financial guarantee for UK £550 per annum when he served as the Under-Secretary to the Government of India, Ministry of Transport, on 07-03-1964. However, despite his position as Director General of Shipping, he was unable to expedite the clearance of my luggage from the customs at the Bombay docks, an area under his office administration. This financial guarantee by Mr. Anand was crucial for my admission to a University in the UK, this is documented with me.

Started Chromatography and Instruments Company.

The creation of the company, Chromatography and Instruments Company, was during my

Ph.D. in 1971. It was during this time that I invented the name, signifying our focus on Chromatography and analytical instruments. I also designed the company's monogram, which symbolised industrial sheds and the gases emanating from chimneys, aligning with the Gas Chromatograph's purpose—to qualitatively and quantitatively analyse gases and smoke emitted by industrial chimneys.

After relocating to Baroda, Gujarat, in 1972, the company was officially registered under the guidance of CA Bipin Shah. The partnership deed was established between Dr. M.K. Shingari and Mr. Shrish Bhailal Bhai Patel of VV Nagar, Anand, formalising our association and shared objectives. This marked the official commencement of our endeavours in the field of chromatography and instrumentation.

Upon the completion of the partnership deed and official registration with the district industry centre in Baroda, our company aimed to secure an industrial plot at GIDC Makarpura. I visited the GIDC office and met the Regional Manager, who coincidentally shared the surname, Patel. I elaborated on my connection with Mr. Shivaganam, the Principal Chief Secretary of Gujarat, mentioning his visit to my university in Swansea and showcasing ongoing research projects, particularly the prototype industrial Gas Chromatograph under my development. Additionally, I highlighted the Indian scholars pursuing their Ph.D. in the Chemistry Department. The Chief Secretary was impressed with our University and suggested that Ph.D. students, upon completion of their studies abroad, should return to India to implement their acquired knowledge. He extended his guidance and support, offering assistance in acquiring an industrial plot or shed in the designated area.

After our discussions, the Regional Manager, Mr. Patel, displayed a high level of cooperation and allocated plots numbered 121 and 122, situated at the main crossroads within GIDC Makarpura. These plots were strategically positioned at the corner, bordered by roads on two sides at the crossroads. On coming out of the Manager's office, individuals awaiting plot allotments queried which plot I had secured. I displayed the allotment letter and they commented favourably on the selection, noting the advantageous positioning with broad roads bordering the plot. Surprisingly, I was unaware of the significance of corner plots or roads adjacent to the plot.

Curiously, they advised me to offer a token of appreciation to the Manager for his favourable gesture. Unfamiliar with the suggestion, I asked for clarification, indicating my education and training from the UK. They advised me to place some money in an envelope and hand it over to the Manager in his office. Following their advice, I enclosed a note of Rs. 10/- in the cover and presented it to the Regional Manager, expressing gratitude for the allocated plot. He glanced inside the envelope, smiled and inquired about who suggested this course of action. I revealed the advice from individuals outside his office. Again, he smiled and said, "Shukriya." This marked my first encounter with bribing a senior Government officer, an unfamiliar practice from my previous experiences.

After approximately 8 to 9 years, Mr. Patel, who held the role of Regional Manager in 1972, returned to Baroda as a Divisional Manager. He reached out to me through the Secretary of the Baroda Chamber of Commerce. Upon my visit to his office in Baroda, I extended my respects and tried to recognise him, unsure if he was the same person who had allocated the plots to me earlier. He graciously offered me a glass of water and then tea. During our interaction, he inquired if I remembered him, to which I regretfully expressed my inability to recall our prior meeting, apologising for my lapse. To my surprise, he retrieved a sealed envelope from his drawer and handed it to me. Upon opening it, I found two currency notes—Rs. 10/- and Rs. 1/-. Perplexed, I questioned him about the purpose of this, to which he explained that it was a return of the same Rs. 10/- I had given him previously, along with an additional rupee as interest. He then recounted the entire story of our previous interaction from 1972. Both of us shared a laugh and parted ways with a handshake. I am delighted to highlight that during 1972, this incident showcased the integrity and honesty prevalent among Gujarat Government officials. Contrastingly, I have learned from an old friend, Mr. Shanti Bhai Patel, since 1972, who is currently engaged in purchasing an old factory, subdividing it into industrial sheds and establishing shops, that is present practice in Government departments now often involve sharing profits in exchange for favours, leading to flourishing business along with Government officials. With the company duly registered and an industrial plot allocated, the design and drawings of the factory shed were approved by

GIDC, permitting us for the construction and only awaiting loan sanction from the Bank of Baroda. We established our account with the GIDC Makarpura Branch of the Bank of Baroda (BOB). With Mr. Shivaganam's assistance, we encountered no issues with BOB. A Cash Credit (CC) Account was opened and a credit limit was sanctioned against the hypothecation of goods. Under the arrangement of hypothecation, we stored raw materials in a designated room where BOB placed its seal and we were obligated not to access the locked goods without the bank's permission and the presence of an authorised officer.

In early 1982, we were availing the facility of hypothecation from BOB. On a particular day, we required some raw materials from the hypothecation store and approached BOB to gain access. Despite multiple visits at 10 A.M., 11:30 A.M. and 01:00 P.M., there was no response to our request. Our entire labour force has been sitting idle since the morning. In a moment of frustration, I instructed my staff to open the store and retrieve the materials we needed. We meticulously prepared a list of the materials removed on this occasion. Around 3:30 P.M., someone from BOB finally arrived and we handed over the list of hypothecated materials that were taken. The officer was visibly upset, started shouting and threatened to close our account. He summoned me to meet the Branch Manager, Mr. Mohit Shah (who is still alive). Mr. Shah, a composed and understanding person, acknowledged that we had made a big mistake by removing the goods without their permission and presence. He informed me that he would forward our case to the Head office for further action. Regrettably, being short-tempered, I expressed my unwillingness to comply and requested the immediate closure of our CC accounts with their bank. Subsequently, the CC account was closed.

The primary objective of our company has always been to design, develop and manufacture highly sophisticated instruments as substitutes for those under embargo from the USA, Japan and Western countries. A significant portion of our instrumentation was purchased by esteemed organisations like BARC, IGCAR, Nuclear Fuel Complex and other Nuclear Industries. During the inception of our Gas Chromatograph (GC) manufacturing, we stood as the sole manufacturing entity in India for Gas Chromatographic instruments. Our Government-approved Research & Development

(R&D) centre also contributed by designing and producing a Hydrogen Determinator for BARC, Tarapur in 1982. This initiative was sparked by Dr. Bhargav, Head, Chemistry Division at BARC Tarapur, who was facing challenges with their Hydrogen Determinators procured from LECO USA via Middle East. These determinators were priced at around 85 lakhs per unit. One of the devices, namely the power supply card, was malfunctioning, while the other provided erratic results. The estimated cost quoted by LECO service engineers for a single power supply PC board was Rs. 85,000/-. However, Dr. Bhargav, a well-experienced Scientist, was aware that the card's cost should not exceed 2-3 thousand rupees. Unwilling to proceed with such a costly order, he sought an alternative from Indian sources.

At that time, we had supplied two laboratory gas chromatographs to his lab, which performed exceptionally well without any interruptions. Dr. Bhargav approached me to develop this Determinator, even though I initially declined, considering the complexity and high cost of the equipment. However, their persistent requests, emphasising the Gas Chromatograph as the core component of the analyser which our company manufactures, are ready for use in the determinator to proceed with designing the furnace. Eventually, he persuaded me. I agreed under the condition that they provide us with a non-functional system or allow us to dismantle a hydrogen Determinator alongside their senior instrumentation and maintenance department.

Dr. Bhargav agreed to dismantle one of their non-working/ nonfunctioning Determinator in their laboratory and granted us a week from Sunday to Friday to study it. We seized this opportunity and successfully designed and manufactured an instrument, with his assurance that he would attempt to procure it if it proved functional. Subsequently, we succeeded in the Determinator project and supplied our first unit to BARC Tarapur at a cost of approximately Rs. 22 lakhs. To date, we manufacture a variety of detectors and we remain the sole manufacturer supplying them to the Atomic Energy establishment.

Participation in Asia-72 Exhibition at Pragati Maidan, New Delhi

In early 1972, Chromatography and Instruments Company received a personal invitation from the "Gujarat Export Corporation Limited" in Ahmedabad, a subsidiary of the Gujarat Government, to participate in the prestigious

International exhibition, “ASIA-72,” expected to be held at Pragati Maidan, New Delhi, during the first week of December 1972. Their Manager conveyed this invitation to us under the instruction of Mr. Rawal, Managing Director of the Gujarat Export Corporation. The suggestion and advice is to exhibit our products in the Gujarat Pavilion through Gujarat Export Corporation as it is the first time they have been manufactured in the country. They assured us of product demonstration and potential order bookings, offering concessional charges for small-scale units. Although I expressed reservations about the attitude of Government officers who participated in exhibitions, Mr. Rawal assured me that our products would be showcased prominently at ASIA-72 as these are import substitute. He even offered reimbursement if we were dissatisfied. We accepted the offer and delivered two of our Gas Chromatographs, captured in a photograph by reporter K.K. Chawla of Hindustan Times on Thursday, December 7, 1972. Notably, Mr. Rawal’s efforts were commendable; he even assigned his daughter, Ms. Alka, as a guide at ASIA-72 to assist in demonstrating how the Gas Chromatography process functioned. During my initial training for two days, Ms. Alka was exceptional — well-mannered, articulate and proficient in explaining our company's product. She dedicated most of her time to our stall as she became very friendly. During the event, there was a press conference hosted at our stall within the Export Corporation, where I shared my candid opinions. The concluding paragraphs of the evening edition of Hindustan Times on December 7, 1972, covered my remarks at the press conference.

"Dr. Shingari expresses gratitude for the support received from the State Government but strongly criticises the bureaucratic hurdles and corruption prevalent at the Central level. He emphasises that these challenges have made it exceedingly difficult for honest and devoted Scientists to thrive in India. Dr. Shingari views these negative factors as detrimental, as they suppress innovation and talent, ultimately contributing to the phenomenon of brain drain. He expresses concern that without the necessary support and resources from the Central authorities to encourage the development of Gas Chromatography, he might also fall victim to this brain drain trend."

"Highlighting the functioning of both the Central and State Government, Dr. Shingari notes that while promises are made during bookings, the authorities tend to overlook concerns once full payments are made. Complaints and grievances are disregarded, left unattended and ultimately brushed under the carpet."

"Following his interview with the Hindustan Times Reporter, several journalists approached me (Dr. Shingari) seeking details about his grievances concerning the Gujarat Export Corporation, with whom the stall was booked. He honestly reported that only 50-60% of the promises made to him were fulfilled and despite his numerous complaints, no action was taken." Dr. Shingari's straightforward views likely appeared in the local newspapers in Delhi. One evening, Mr. Rawal, the Managing Director of Gujarat Export Corporation, approached me (Dr. Shingari) and offered a full refund if he was dissatisfied, assuring that his equipment would be retained for the full period of the exhibition and returned to Ahmedabad afterwards. Consequently, Dr. Shingari felt compelled to remain silent and ceased further complaints regarding the lack of facilities.

A copy of the press cutting detailing his experience is enclosed in the appendix.

I want to emphasize here that my approach and principle are still unchanged as it was in 1972. These principles and attitutes have persisted over the time, shaped by my background in RSS and imbibed imbibed from British discipline in both his personal and professional life.

Marriage with Dr. Kiran Vohra

Upon my return from the UK, I found myself at the age of 28, a young man ready for marriage. The year 1972 was a whirlwind of activities as I immersed myself in establishing a company dedicated to manufacturing cutting-edge instruments that our country was importing. Unknown to me, the resounding demand of our honourable Prime Minister, Shri Narendra Bhai Damodardas Modi, to “MAKE IN INDIA” became a prominent slogan in the subsequent years, starting on September 25, 2014. In my case, I had already embarked on the journey of “MAKE IN INDIA” in 1972-1973. We successfully designed and manufactured our initial product, the Gas Chromatograph, both in England and India, marking the inception of this concept. I can proudly claim to be 42 years ahead of our esteemed PM Modi ji.

Our commitment to “MAKE IN INDIA” began in 1972, during Modi Ji’s tenure as Chief Minister of Gujarat. I wouldn't hesitate to assert that our company pioneered the concept long before it became a National Slogan. It would be worthwhile to bring this to the attention of our honourable PM Modi ji.

Amidst my dedication to establishing the company and formulating future plans, my focus on the marriage front was limited. Shuttling between Baroda, Ahmedabad, Gandhinagar and New Delhi left me with little time to actively seek a life partner. I entrusted the task to my parents, elder sisters and friends, outlining three non-negotiable conditions for my marriage:

1. No dowry or gifts.
2. A simple ceremony in any temple, preferably an Arya Samaj temple.
3. No grand procession; a direct transition from the temple to our home after the marriage ceremony.

My family members, including my father, sisters, younger brother and other relatives, very firmly rejected the aforementioned conditions for my marriage. Consequently, they withdrew from the task of seeking a suitable match for me. With familial options exhausted, my close friends, such as D.P. Gupta, Hari Bijlani, Vinod Sood and Bhisham Kohli, took on the responsibility of finding a suitable match. D.P. Gupta emerged as the most capable among them, being married to a young lady who was a Gold medallist in history from Delhi University and worked as a lecturer at the same university. She was the daughter of a serving Colonel in the Indian Army and resided in South Delhi. Our decision was to publish an advertisement in the local newspaper, Hindustan Times.

Numerous responses poured in from Northern India and we shortlisted two suitable ladies, one from Gwalior and the other from Varanasi. Concurrently, our company was actively participating in the ASIA-72 exhibition, a month-long event where I played a pivotal role in managing our stall and presenting to interested parties. Routine visitor interactions were handled by a lady guide, Miss Alka Jani, as evident from the press cutting/clip dated December 7, 1972. Despite my busy schedule, we initiated correspondence with the two families from Gwalior and Varanasi.

Gwalior Case:

Our correspondence commenced with the father of the young lady, who held a postgraduate degree in applied arts and worked from home. She had a brother, an artist residing in America, specialising in writing children's books. Her father, Mr. Dabur, was an industrialist involved in cold storage and other businesses, also serving as the President of the Rotary Club of Gwalior. His wife was well-educated and held the position of president at the Inner Wheel Lady Rotary Club.

Mr. Dabur visited our ASIA-72 exhibition stall and invited me to visit their family in Gwalior. Since my family wasn't supportive, I travelled to Gwalior by night train, checked into a pre-booked 3-star hotel. Mr. Dabur picked me up the next morning and I spent a considerable amount of time with the lady and her family. Despite my family's absence and my three conditions, I found the lady to be simple and agreeable and Mr. Dabur seemed straightforward. However, her mother was talkative and inquired about my family's absence. I responded honestly, which led to some discomfort. After lunch, they left me at my hotel.

That evening, my cousin, Mr. Ravi Sarin, expressed a desire to meet the family. When I conveyed this to Mrs. Dabur, her response was rude, stating that her daughter is not a tamasha for anyone to come and see. Displeased, I declined further interest. My cousin investigated and found the family to be respected and affluent. I returned to Delhi the next morning instead of taking my originally booked evening train.

To my surprise, Mr. Dabur visited the exhibition again, apologising for his wife's behaviour. He insisted that his daughter approved of me and was willing to stay in my one-room apartment. He openly accepted me and urged reconsideration. I agreed to meet in Baroda. Later, an emissary from Mr. Narhari Amin's office, an MP and prominent businessman, visited, suggesting a small bungalow as an alternative. I declined, stating my preference for my one-room apartment. Despite a subsequent letter from Mr. Dabur expressing a desire to visit Baroda, I chose not to respond, as my decision was influenced by the unfavourable impression of Mrs. Dabur, adhering to the belief, "*Jaisi Maa – Tessi Beti*," and ultimately rejecting the proposal.

Varanasi Case:

Our Varanasi matrimonial journey began in Connaught Place, New Delhi when a gentleman named Kumar Chopra responded to my matrimonial advertisement in Hindustan Times. He introduced himself as the nephew of Prof. Dwarka Nath Vohra, the Professor and Head of the Political Science Department at Banaras Hindu University, Varanasi. Mr. Chopra conveyed my details to Prof. Vohra and discussed my educational and family background. During our conversation, he inquired about my plans to settle in India or return to the UK. I affirmed my commitment to settling in India without any intention of returning to the UK.

Subsequently, a meeting was arranged in Delhi in the first week of October 1972 at Mr. Anand's, a close family friend of Prof. Vohra, residence in Greater Kailash, South Delhi, with Prof. Vohra and Mrs. Vohra. My friends, Mrs. and Mr. Davender Gupta, were present alongside me. Prof. Vohra shared that he, too, had been educated in the UK, earning his Ph.D. degree from Cambridge University. After a lengthy discussion, his final question revolved around my business experience. I honestly stated that I had none but possessed a Ph.D. degree and could secure a job anywhere. I explained that I left Swansea University after receiving positive signals from the external examiner and my professor, indicating the successful completion of my Ph.D.. I had received the official result in India and was confident in my ability to succeed in business.

During our conversation, Prof. Vohra's wife expressed a desire to meet my parents. I respectfully explained that my mother had passed away in 1963, six months after my departure to the UK. Prof. Vohra immediately inquired if I had returned for her funeral, to which I replied that financial constraints and a lack of a suitable job in England had prevented my return. I emphasised my commitment in achieving my goal before returning to India.

Prof. Vohra questioned the likelihood of my success in business due to my lack of business experience, financial constraints and my uncompromising attitude. I responded that if I failed, I would return to the UK as there was an open offer from the HOD of the Chemical Engineering department at Swansea University. Prof. Vohra continued to probe, asking about the location of the marriage, whether in Varanasi or Delhi, how much money I intended to draw from the company for household expenses and how confident I was in competing with foreign companies in the UK, USA and Japan. He also inquired about any conditions I had in mind.

I responded under,

1. Marriage will take place in any temple in Delhi

2. The following are uncompromisable conditions from my side

    - No Dowry, no gifts.
    - Simple marriage in any temple, preferably Arya Samaj Temple
    - No Barat and after the ceremony, I will proceed to our house in Lajpat Nagar straight from the temple with my wife.

3. I will be drawing Rs. 350/- per month and staying in one one-room apartment. We will maintain our house with this budget.

Prof. Vohra was not convinced at all that anyone having Ph.D. and after 9 – 10 years of stay in the UK, how can he run the house with this meagre amount? In front of me, he asked Mrs. Vohra two questions:

Can anyone run the house with Rs. 350/- per month?

Do you think your daughter can live in one room and manage a house with Rs. 350/-?

Mrs. Vohra expressed that the decision to proceed was ultimately upto Kiran. She believed that managing with the specified budget was possible. Following this, they invited me to pose any questions I might have. I responded affirmatively, expressing a desire to meet Kiran and understand each other's attitudes and expectations before proceeding further.

After my meeting with Mr. and Mrs. Vohra, I formed the impression that Prof. Vohra might prefer his daughter to marry someone in a foreign country like Europe or the USA. He seemed unconvinced about my ability to succeed in business in India and anticipated potential failure.

A few days later, Mr. Kumar Chopra, owner of a domestic cylinder manufacturing company in Faridabad, contacted me through Mr. D.P. Gupta for another meeting. During our meeting at Mr. Anand's residence in Greater Kailash, attended by myself, Mrs. and Mr. Gupta, Prof. Vohra, Mrs. Vohra and their daughter, Miss. Kiran Vohra, we engaged in general discussions over tea. I inquired about Kiran's Ph.D. research work, learning about her ongoing thesis work and the delay caused by the computer awaiting results from IIT, Kanpur, using their advanced computer facility.

I suggested moving to another room for a more private conversation and despite Kiran's refusal to go outside, we discussed our past and future in detail. Kiran agreed to manage the house with a budget of Rs. 350 per month and live in a single room. She expressed her willingness to reside wherever I chose to live after marriage, even if it meant resigning from her temporary lecturership at the Women's College of BHU once she obtained her Ph.D. in Electronics from IIT.

I shared my educational background including completing my B.Sc. Hons., M.Sc. and Ph.D. in Chemical Engineering in England and asked if she wanted to know about my past relationships. Kiran declined, stating she was not interested in my past. I also informed her about my family's non-approval due to my specified conditions and she assured me that she could manage and handle them with my help.

Returning to the main group after our private discussion, Mrs. Gupta also assessed Kiran's mental set-up. Despite everyone else appearing happy and positive, Prof. Vohra seemed less convinced, giving the impression that he believed our marriage might not succeed. Nonetheless, we decided to proceed and Mrs. Vohra asked about the timeline for the wedding, to which I responded within a maximum of 15 days.

On November 10, 1972, Mr. Chopra contacted me through Mr. D.P. Gupta for a meeting at his office in Connaught Place. During the meeting, Mr. Chopra suggested I start my company in Faridabad instead of Baroda, Gujarat. He cited his connections in Delhi, Punjab and Haryana and his influence with prominent figures like Haryana's CM, Mr. Bansi Lal and PM Indira Gandhi Ji. I politely declined and Mr. Chopra, upset with my decision, expressed his displeasure. He conveyed that he would brief his views to his Mama Ji in Varanasi and indicated that his family might not agree. I remained firm in my decision and left his office.

After this meeting, it was discussed that Mr. Chopra's behaviour might be influenced by instructions from Prof. Vohra, who seemed uninterested in having his daughter marry me due to my conditions, my firm attitude and my family's financial condition. Upon careful consideration, I wrote a letter to Miss Kiran Vohra explaining my difficulties in marrying her, citing her father's concerns and my family's hesitation. I received a letter from Kiran expressing her commitment and stating that she had no intention of going abroad. She mentioned her sister's dissatisfaction with life in England and her advice against marrying someone from a foreign settler. Despite these letters, I decided to decline the proposal.

After a week, I received another letter from Kiran, urging me to tell Kiran's fault and emphasising that punishing her due to misunderstandings with others was unjust. Unable to find an answer, I ultimately gave my consent and we decided to marry before the end of November. I received a phone call from Mr. D.P. Gupta, informing me that they were coming to Delhi and would stay with the Anand family and a date and time were fixed for our meeting.

During the second week of November, we all, from my side and from Kiran's side, met at Mr. Anand's residence at 11 A.M. Kiran's elder sister, Dr. Malti Sarin from the UK, was also present in the meeting. Dr. Malti Sarin had a long chat with me about my education at Glamorgan College of Technology, Treforest, after learning about my performance in the final year of my B.Sc. Hons. in Chemical Engineering, second position in the class, an award from Imperials Smelting Corporation and several letters of appreciation from HOD and other professors. She also realised that on the basis of these recommendation letters and testimonials, I was offered a place in the M.Sc. in Chemical Engineering programme at Swansea College of the University of Wales. When she came to know that I was getting a full grant plus fees during my post-graduation and Ph.D. work at the University, she was very impressed with my credentials and my personality. She was full of praise for me. She fully approved and found me most suitable for her younger sister. I noticed that all of Vohra's family were very happy except Prof. Vohra. Dr. Malti Sarin asked me about how I felt about her sister and this alliance. I told her "As far as your sister Kiran is concerned, she is acceptable and I feel we both will be able to get along comfortably as we both are very straightforward and do not hide anything". Since Malti Sarin was in the UK for many decades, she was very Frank and asked me whether I had girlfriends at my college and University. I said many during my college days and none while doing my Ph.D.. She asked why so; my answer was that I had been working from 18 – 20 hours per day and fully involved in my research work. There was no time at all for anything except to work hard and complete my Ph.D. before grants expired. With this attitude, I could complete my project within two years against an allocated period of 3 years. Her last question was what Kiran would do after marriage. "She will work with me at the company without losing time" was my instant reply. She asked jokingly how you would treat her – like a wife or like a friend. I told her I believed in friendship and that's why I had many girlfriends during my graduation. She gave a good smile and openly said "Mahender is very suitable for her and I fully approve".

After this, we had good refreshments and fixed 29th November for the marriage. Dr. Sarin asked Mrs. and Mr. Gupta, a Senior Engineer at DESU and Mrs. Gupta, a lecturer at Delhi University, to have information about the Mandir's location and time. I intervened and told them that I would prefer Arya Samaj Mandir. Mr. Gupta managed to fix one Arya Samaj Mandir at Hanuman Road near Connaught Place and the time fixed was 10 A.M. Myself and my friends left Mr. Anand's house and informed the date of marriage to our family members. No invitation cards were printed and I was telling all the friends who were coming in contact with me that I was getting married on 29th November, 1972 at 10 A.M. at Arya Samaj Mandir, Hanuman Road. I invited them to join the marriage. The whole day I was busy with the exhibition and I could contact very few friends. None of my friends turned up, as everybody took it very lightly and thought I was pulling their legs. They knew I was very busy with the exhibition, so I was not expecting that I would get married in November during the exhibition period. From our side, we were four people – My father, two brothers and one sister. My elder brother and sister were in the UK. From Vohra's family, there were around twenty participants, including Dr. Malti Sarin. The marriage took place at 10 A.M. and it was over by 11 A.M. Tea plus a few snacks were served there and the whole function was over by 1 o'clock in the afternoon... I paid Rs. 5/- to Pandit Ji and Rs. 17/- to the taxi to take us to our home at Lajpat Nagar. Kiran became Kiran Shingari and joined our family. I had one day off from the exhibition and stayed at home to introduce Kiran to my other relatives and friends living near our home. Kiran and I stayed in the house and in the evening, we all 4 – Mr. and Mrs. Gupta and two of us went to the public garden near our house. Before going to the garden, we went to the Central Market and had some snacks. After that, we located a peaceful corner of the garden and sat there. Gupta's gave Kiran very practical and sincere advice in the form of incidents and experiences of their honeymoon night. His family conditions were similar to mine.

Mr. Gupta was brought up by his mother and lived in one room apartment in Amar colony, a refugee colony; his family details, etc. I have already mentioned it in earlier chapters, but I am still summarising it here. After he became a Junior Engineer at the Government department, he decided to get married. He was very financially weak, had no house and had to take care of her mother, two sisters and one brother; apart from many distant relatives, all came from Pakistan. He seriously thought that he must have a wife who cooperated and shared the responsibilities of bringing up his family. He located a working lady who was a lecturer at Delhi University. She was a Gold medallist and because of her results, she got the job immediately after passing out from the same University. Her father was a working Colonel. She had a chicken pox scar on her face and because of that, she was not getting any suitable match. Gupta selected her after she agreed to join him to upbring his family. On the first night, he took her to the garden and sat there peacefully. He told his wife "There is a very big difference between both the families. You are the only daughter of a Colonel and the whole family is educated, well-placed in society and living in very comfortable accommodations. On the contrary, I am a refugee and now we are a very poor family. I am the only earning member, i.e. I am the breadwinner. I have to take care of my old mother, who is illiterate and brought me up by working as a domestic help in various houses. My father was killed during the partition of India in 1947. My younger sisters and brothers are all dependent on me. On the contrary, you are a Gold medallist from Delhi University and got a good job there. There is no comparison between you and my mother. She will not be able to understand you, but you still have to understand and manage to get along with her. If a situation arises, one has to leave the house, it will be you as you can go to your father's house and my mother has no place to go. In view of this, I suggest and request that you get in touch with her. Also, she will make many mistakes because of her educational background; you have to learn to ignore them and control the situation. I am always with you and you can bank upon my support with you." This marked the honeymoon period for Davender Gupta and Sulakshna Gupta, a time of newly wed bliss.

After sharing the story of their first night together, they offered ten pieces of advice to us, which they believed were essential for navigating familial dynamics:

1. First Advice - Always show respect by touching the feet of any senior individuals who visit you or your home.

2. Offer Hospitality - Offer refreshments like tea to guests, even if they decline initially. Politely insist a few times and maintain humility by keeping your eyes lowered.

3. Companionship - Mahender will refrain from going to the exhibition for the next two days to be with you.

4. Avoid Gossip - After paying respects and offering tea to elderly female visitors, refrain from sitting with them under the pretext of attending to house- hold tasks.

5. Anticipate Drama - Expect that family members will attempt to poison Mahender's mind after his return from the exhibition. This may involve complaints about you, leading to Mahender scolding you. Both of you are expected to engage in this drama.

6. Endure Criticism - Endure Mahender's harsh words and scolding in front of family members, shedding false tears. After a few days, family members will sympathise with you and accept you.

7. Enjoy Together - Once you have met all your relatives, Mahender will take you to the exhibition, where you can spend quality time together.

8. Seek Support - The next morning, touch the feet of all family members before hurrying to the kitchen. Mahender's father will likely approach you, sympathise with your situation and assure you that Mahender's behaviour is not unusual. If the mistreatment persists, inform him and he will intervene.

9. Maintain Seriousness - Avoid cracking jokes or laughing in front of family members and relatives. Maintain a composed outward behaviour similar to Dilip Kumar's serious expressions.

10. Gain Sympathy - After a few days of this drama, family members and relatives will begin to sympathise with you and speak highly of you.

This advice, though unconventional, was believed by Davender and Sulakshna Gupta to be crucial for navigating the intricacies of familial relationships during the early stages of marriage.

The set of ten pieces of advice from Mrs. and Mr. Gupta proved to be remarkably effective, leading Kiran to become the most esteemed daughter-in-law in our family. Her conduct and demeanour earned her immense respect and favour among all family members, establishing a win-win situation for everyone involved. It became evident that Mahender's decision to choose Kiran as his life partner was indeed wise and beneficial for all.

Kiran actively started accompanying Mahender to the exhibition on a regular basis, returning with him as well. Mahender ensured that his family members were informed of Kiran's active participation and technical proficiency at the exhibition. He highlighted her contributions and emphasised her capability to assist him not only at the exhibition but also in their future venture of owning a factory in Baroda. The family's support and encouragement were essential for their successful transition from Delhi to Baroda as they embarked on this new entrepreneurial journey.

At the exhibition, our stall was overseen by Miss Alka, the daughter of the Managing Director of Gujarat Export Corporation, who served as a guide. Despite being an MA student at Baroda University, she took on the role of a guide as a seasonal job. Right from the outset, Miss Alka displayed a friendly demeanour towards me, showing genuine interest and care. During seminars and lectures, she often sat beside me, demonstrating attentiveness and consideration. Even after introducing Kiran as my wife, Miss Alka's behaviour remained unchanged, indicating her continued interest in me. Although Kiran may have felt uncomfortable at times, she maintained her composure. Miss Alka's intelligence, open-mindedness, punctuality and fluency in multiple languages, including Hindi, Gujarati and English, were evident throughout our interactions.

As the exhibition came to a close, we took great care in packing our Gas Chromatographs into secure boxes behind our stall, intending to transport them to Baroda. However, we encountered a restriction preventing us from removing anything from the exhibition venue without the appropriate passes issued only to stall owners. Consequently, we were informed that we could retrieve our instruments from their office in Ahmedabad, necessitating a different approach to transport them back home.

My wife Kiran's Ph.D. Thesis

My wife, Kiran and I embarked on a journey to Varanasi, where she had conducted her research for her Ph.D. in Electronics. Her thesis was supervised by Dr. P.K. Mishra from Physics Department, who had completed his own Doctorate under Prof. Banerjee. Despite Prof. Banerjee's relocation to Kolkata after retirement, he instructed Dr. Mishra to assist Kiran with her research. However, there seemed to be delays in forwarding Kiran's thesis to Prof. Banerjee for approval and the appointment of an external examiner, despite Prof. Mishra's familiarity with Prof. D.N. Vohra, Kiran's father, who facilitated the introduction.

Upon my introduction to Prof. Mishra through Kiran's father, I inquired about the delays in processing Kiran's thesis. Dr. Mishra cited technical issues as the reason for the delay and was hesitant to forward the thesis. I requested a copy of the thesis so I could review it myself. After spending two weeks meticulously examining her thesis, I identified grammatical errors and suggested changes to the presentation of diagrams and tables. At a subsequent meeting at our home, I shared my findings and recommendations with Dr. Mishra. While he acknowledged the corrections, he expressed concerns about the thesis's results, noting a discrepancy with his own Ph.D. work.

I decided to contact Prof. Banerjee in Kolkata, explaining my engineering Ph.D. background from the University of Wales, UK and the discussions with Dr. Mishra. Prof. Banerjee agreed that identical results were not imperative and proposed upgrading the programme and running it on the powerful computer at IIT Kanpur. If the results were comparable, he suggested concluding the thesis and officially submitting it for review. During our discussions, I emphasised to Prof. Banerjee the importance of a Ph.D. candidate's ability to independently solve problems within their project.

Over the course of four months, we revised the thesis and submitted it to Prof. Banerjee. He arranged for an external examiner familiar to him, who approved the thesis, enabling Kiran to obtain her Ph.D. Despite the challenges and disagreements with Dr. Mishra, Kiran successfully completed her Ph.D. without the full support of her acting supervisor.

In the 1973 convocation held at Banaras Hindu University, Varanasi, Mrs. Kiran Shingari was conferred with the title of Dr. Mrs. Kiran Shingari, having earned her Doctorate degree.

Summary

Section 5: The Glorious Years - 1972 to 1975

Major incidents:

1. Instrumentation Company in Gujarat.
2. Participation in the International Industrial Exhibition ASIA 1972.
3. Marriage – The most beautiful turning point of my life.
4. Manufacturing of GC. Purchase of land in GIDC, Vadodara and construction of CIC factory.

Learning:

1. To develop, design and manufacture highly sophisticated instruments is not the objective of the company, but it's the image and mission to be followed as a legacy.
2. Principles and attitudes have persisted over the time, shaped by the RSS and British Discipline, encounters during the process of learning.

3. Conditions play a very important role in one's life – whether it's in professional life or Personal life.

Chapter defining quote:

"The progress in professional life has a major impact in building up the image at a personal front."

Section 6
Dreams Now Converted into Reality

"As I look back at the journey of my life, my most impactful years set an example for others."

Eventful Years 1973-74

The year 1972 stands as a significant milestone in my career and its reverberations continued into 1973, a year filled with events that left an indelible mark on both my professional and personal life. A noteworthy addition to my life during this period was the expansion of my family with the birth of my son, Gaurav. This joyous occasion brought a new layer of responsibility, blending seamlessly with my professional pursuits.

Concurrently, another pivotal development unfolded as construction work commenced on the premises of our company. This marked the beginning of the creation of a physical space that would serve as the nucleus of our operations—a space that would witness the growth and progress of our venture. A crucial milestone during this period was the initiation of the manufacturing process for Gas Chromatographs (GC). This marked a significant phase in our business operations, underscoring our commitment to provide high-quality, domestically manufactured instruments—a testament to our dedication to the "Make in India" ethos.

Moreover, technological advancements played a vital role in shaping our capabilities. Plans were set in motion to acquire the technology of Recorder and Electron Capture Detector (ECD) in the near future. The integration of these three components would complete our GC system, enhancing its functionality and efficiency. The detailed records of these significant events is provided below.

Expansion of family

Following our marriage, our attention turned towards the upcoming exhibition and we devised a plan for me to visit and follow up with potential clients who had shown interest during ASIA-72, New Delhi. My journey covered the states of UP, Bihar, Punjab and Haryana before heading to Baroda or Varanasi. This allowed me to personally understand their applications and requirements. Meanwhile, Kiran spent quality time with my family and relatives. Subsequently, Kiran and I headed to Varanasi, where the plan was for her to stay with her parents until suitable accommodation was arranged for our residence. It was during this period that Kiran became pregnant, prompting us to make collective decisions about family planning. We opted to have two children in succession, aiming for them to grow up together, attend school simultaneously and be cared for by Kiran while I managed the factory and the business. Our first child, a son named Gaurav, entered the world on October 5, 1973, followed by our second son, Amar, born on April 1, 1975, with a gap of one and a half years between them.

Gaurav

Amar

In the initial years of our business, from 1973 to 1975, my responsibilities often kept me away from home as I travelled to cities like Ahmedabad,

Gandhinagar, Bombay and Delhi. The primary purpose of these travels was to oversee tasks related to designing and constructing the factory shed, securing finances for construction and exploring potential trial orders from established contacts. Due to my frequent travel, we decided that Kiran would stay with her parents until our child was 2-3 months old. This decision was well received, especially by Prof. Vohra, Kiran's father.

I would like to mention here that from my childhood, I could not tolerate injustice, misbehaviour and corruption. During my younger days, when I owned Amar Hotel in Kota, in January 1974, I, along with my wife and 4-month-old son Gaurav, was returning from Kota to Baroda by the morning train. We could not get a confirmed reservation. I boarded the reserved secondclass compartment, hoping to get at least one reserved seat for my wife and child. On the way, I requested ticket inspector Mr. Trivedi to allot us the berth by taking extra charges with a penalty to continue my journey as my son was only four months old.

He answered that there was no seat available and we better get down at the next station. I further requested him to please see if he could allot me a seat in the first class. His answer was negative. I then told him that he had been allotting seats to other unreserved passengers in front of everybody, asking me to get down at the next station. On getting exposed, he reacted that I should get down from the running train. Seeing the unethical and inhuman behaviour, I got up and held his neck in both hands and told him that he was a very corrupt and inhuman person; I would lodge his complaint at the next station. He halted the train by pulling the chain, called RPF and asked them to lodge his complaint of strangling him in front of all the passengers. He also asked another passenger to sign as a witness, but nobody came forward. Instead, they were telling him that he should have given us at least one seat while travelling with a small baby. He did not listen to anyone and asked the police to take me into custody. The police arrested me. Then I told TTE Mr. Trivedi that I owned my hotel in Kota and that I regularly travel on this route. Let me come out from police custody, as the police cannot hold me for long and then I will show you my power. In the meantime, one of my employees, Mr. Parkhi, ex-army personnel, was also in the unreserved compartment of the train. Since the train was halted there for about half an hour and our Engineer came out and on seeing what was happening, he involved himself in this episode. But I told him to take my wife to Baroda and I also told my wife to phone Railway Minister Mr. Kamlapati Tripathi, who happens to be a very close friend of my father-in-law, Prof. D.N. Vohra. After hearing all that, the police also suggested TTE to withdraw the complaint.

It seems he got scared and finally withdrew his complaint. We travelled in the same compartment and reached Baroda half an hour late without paying any extra amount or penalty, which I had offered initially. In January 1974, I brought both of them to Baroda to our one-room apartment in GIDC colony. Simultaneously, we purchased two apartments in the company's name, with one serving as our residence and the other occupied by my partner, Mr. Shrish Patel and his wife. Upon moving into our apartment, we faced the challenge of arranging a suitable sleeping arrangement. The idea of buying a double bed was discarded due to high costs. Instead, I recycled wooden planks from wooden boxes which contained my luggage, which I had brought from England, to create two box-type beds with ample storage space. These beds, crafted in 1974, continue to be in use in our present house in 2024.

In June 1974, my wife conceived again, leading to the decision to shift her along with Gaurav to Varanasi. This move was driven by the lack of accommodation and facilities to accommodate our growing family. This decision received widespread appreciation from our relatives and friends. Both children were born in Varanasi and during my travels to IIT Kanpur, HBIT Kanpur and Agriculture University Kanpur, all of which eventually became our customers, I would visit them. Our initial order for GC came from Banaras Hindu University, where Prof. Vohra served as the HOD of the Political Science department and Chief warden for Birla Hostel.

Our second son, Amar, was born on April 1, 1975. Kiran remained in Varanasi with the children until August 14, when she moved to Baroda. We celebrated Independence Day as a family, marking a special moment in our lives as we shared the joy in our double-plus (king-size) bed—the first home we called our own. Our initial residence was a C-type one-room flat, where we cherished life for about 4-5 years before transitioning to a B-type row house.

It's noteworthy that our C-type apartment was on the ground floor and we were fortunate to have surplus land in front and on the side. Despite financial constraints, I was passionate about greenery and plants. Despite the stony nature of the land, it is often used for the storage of construction materials and dumping of waste materials. I fenced the surplus area and transformed it into a remarkable flower and vegetable garden. This garden became a distinctive feature of the C-type housing. GIDC authorities would showcase our garden to senior officers visiting from Ahmedabad and Gandhinagar.

My passion for gardening faced challenges when neighbours began encroaching on the extra land attached to the apartments, using it as a dump yard or for temporary structures. Executive Engineers and Junior Engineers from GIDC, upon noticing unauthorised land use, issued orders for removal. While most complied, I persisted in maintaining my garden and lawn, enjoying evenings and dinners there. Despite clashes with GIDC's Assistant Engineer, who dismantled the fencing, I consistently restored it. Eventually, they acknowledged the aesthetic value and allowed the garden to thrive, recognising its contribution to the apartment's overall appearance.

Upon moving to B-type quarters, where we owned five flats, we continued our passion for gardening. We created gardens at the back, on one side and the front of the apartments. We still possess these five apartments in a block of ten. To provide shade, filter air and enhancing the surroundings, I planted numerous trees on the front and side of the building, considering it a corner plot. At the back, we preserved a large green space, following the original plan of the colony.

Since we owned five apartments in proximity, I requested GIDC town planner to include the area in our ownership, allowing us to convert it into a green garden. This request was granted and we developed a garden, complete with a small swimming pool that our staff residing there still enjoys. This commitment to nature spans five decades, reflecting my belief in the green revolution and proactive efforts to transform unused land into lush greenery. It's gratifying to see such initiatives gaining momentum and alignment with contemporary environmental initiatives implemented by the Government.

An intriguing incident unfolded during the allotment of B-type accommodations in GIDC colony. The GIDC had designated B-type apartments for the owners of the company and C-type residences for the workers, each allocated under individual names. Unfortunately, the majority of C-type houses suffered from substandard construction, leading to severe leakage issues during the monsoon season. Despite numerous complaints from the residents to the GIDC, no action was taken to rectify the situation. The workers, facing hardships, sought my assistance, considering our company owned many houses in both B and C types.

On holiday, we decided to form an association comprising the house owners of GIDC colony.

This association represented the General Manager of GIDC, who resided in B-type tenements. Despite the Manager's recommendation to the Regional Manager in Ahmedabad, no actions were initiated. Frustrated by the lack of response, the association appointed me as the President and granted me the authority to take necessary actions. Our meetings were held after 8 P.M., following dinner, where joint decisions were made.

To address the issue, I proposed that we collectively cease paying the regular instalments to GIDC. The houses were initially provided on an instalment basis to encourage people to settle in GIDC and establish factories, fostering development in the area. When GIDC higher authorities learned that no one was paying instalments, Junior Engineers and the contractor who constructed the buildings approached me, requesting a resolution. They promised to rectify all the houses, a process that would take about six months or more for over 100 apartments. They proposed an immediate fix for my house, if I assisted them in persuading residents to resume instalment payments.

My response was firm—I insisted that they attend to my house last after repairing all the C-type houses in the colony. Even the General

Manager, residing in the same colony, approached me and I reiterated my stance. Repair work began with C-type quarters and concluded with my five apartments, which fortunately had no remaining issues. With the guidance of Jr. Engineer Mr. Christian, who is still a friend of mine enjoying retirement in Baroda, I managed to resolve our problems using my materials. In 1990, we relocated to our company's guest house at 333-334, GIDC Makarpura, known as "Parishram." The story of Parishram is detailed at the end of this chapter under the heading "Parishram in Doctor & Doctor."

Construction of CIC Factory Building

In 1973, the Chromatography and Instruments Company's blueprint secured approval from the Baroda Municipal Corporation (BMC). The initial phase of construction involved the creation of two rooms, each measuring 16 ft. x 15 ft., designated for office and production purposes. The design incorporated reinforced concrete (RCC) structures. The approved plan outlined two halls, each spanning around 2000 sq. ft., bringing the total area to 4000 sq. ft. Within the first hall, two rooms of approximately 240-250 sq. ft. each were designated for office and laboratory purposes. However, we repurposed the second room to serve as a production or assembly room instead of a laboratory.

Both rooms in the first hall featured a False ceiling at a height of 10 ft., while the industrial room stood at a height of 14 ft. The front hall served as an assembly hall, while the second hall was utilised as a mechanical workshop. The current configuration of the halls remains the same. The original building was constructed with a beams and column structure in 1973, comprising only a ground floor.

Over the time, it has evolved into a ground-plus three-storey RCC structure, with the top floor featuring brick walls and a galvanised sheet ceiling. Presently, the facility boasts six halls across the ground, first and second floors, with a combined hall on the top floor. Remarkably, from its inception in 1972 to the present-day, the company has consistently reported profits in its balance sheets, with the profit margin progressively increasing each year. Importantly, the upper three stories of the building were constructed using the company's profits and no loans were sought for this purpose.

Photograph of this building is shown above

Second Building

Manufacturing of Gas Chromatograph(GC)

The initial phase involved establishing our office and commencing the enhancement of Gas Chromatography (GC) systems that I had imported from England and showcased at ASIA-72. After disassembling the prototype, we fabricated and applied a new coat of paint to the outer housing of the GC, presenting it with a polished and professional appearance. These two GC systems, with their newly painted housing, were then displayed at ASIA-72.

By the later part of 1973, we had initiated the manufacturing process for sub-assemblies of Thermal Conductivity Detector (TCD) GC and Flame Ionisation Detector (FID) GC. Critical components such as the TCD & FID Detectors, GC Columns and Injection Syringes were imported from England along with our luggage. However, the remaining components, including the injector and gas control system, needed to be produced locally. We procured the necessary parts for gas control, such as needle valves, pressure gauges and small-diameter tubing, from the Bombay Market. An additional challenge arose as we lacked access to carrier gases like Nitrogen, Hydrogen and Air, essential for testing and operating the GCs. Indian Oxygen Limited was the exclusive company manufacturing these gases and control regulators, but their rental terms proved to be restrictive. Despite these challenges in obtaining the required gases, we pressed on with the production process. To address the testing challenge, our partner, Mr. Patel, who hailed from Vallabh Vidyanagar, I leveraged his father, Bhailal Bhai's connections with the Vice-Chancellor and Head of Chemistry Department at Vallabh Vidyanagar University. An unofficial arrangement was made with the Head of Chemistry department to facilitate the testing of our GC systems. Official correspondence was generated, proposing demonstrations of our TCD-GC and FID-GC to the Chemistry department and other relevant departments. A consensus was reached that if the performance of our GCs matched that of foreign models, the University would consider purchasing them, contingent on approval. This strategic arrangement allowed us to circumvent testing and calibration at our factory. Despite not having a recording device, specifically a Potentiometric Strip Chart Recorder, we positioned ourselves as GC manufacturers, emphasising that recorders and gas cylinders were items available for purchase from specialised manufacturers.

With the invaluable assistance of the Chemistry department at V V Nagar University, we successfully calibrated and tested the GCs by December 1973, preparing them for demonstration purposes only, as we retained them for our reference. Our primary objective was to assess the quality and reliability of Indian components for optimal performance.

Importing raw materials for GC production was very expensive due to a customs duty of 350%. This duty would significantly inflate the price of Indian-made GCs, making them unattractive to potential buyers. Moreover, without an import licence, importing materials was practically impossible and any attempt would result in confiscation. Despite these challenges, we decided to forge ahead, concentrating on GCs with a TCD detector only.

The TCD's sensor utilised tungsten filaments, an imported item from the USA. To overcome this obstacle, we ingeniously repurposed tungsten filaments from light bulbs by breaking the glass and extracting the filaments for use in the detector cavity. This resourceful approach allowed us to develop a functional TCD. We successfully manufactured two GCs based on TCD, with the only drawback being the shorter lifespan of our filament compared to the imported version. However, our main priority at this stage was introducing our GCs to the market, even if they utilised bulb filaments. The TCD-GC required only one carrier gas—Hydrogen Gas—instead of the three gases required for testing and operating the Flame Ionisation Detector in other models. Consequently, we shifted our focus to TCD-based GC systems.

Our gratitude extends to the Chemistry department and their Vice-Chancellor for permitting us to utilise their testing facilities for both TCD and FID systems. We successfully developed and manufactured the Indian version of the TCD-based Gas Chromatograph, predominantly using Indian components and introduced it to the market in 1974.

Between 1974 and 1975, we directed our efforts toward FID-GC. We possessed one FID-based system from England and one from India. The original system was offered to the Chemistry department of the National Chemical Laboratory (NCL) in Hyderabad. The head of the department, a distinguished scientist named Dr. Subha Rao, placed a trial order, subject to the GC working satisfactorily in his laboratory for 30 days. After a successful operation for a month, he recommended it to the store purchase department and we accepted the order. However, after 12 stable performances, the system suddenly began to exhibit erratic behaviour on the second day, severely impacting its performance. Despite our disappointment and confusion, Dr. Subha Rao consoled us and assured us that these issues could be resolved. We obtained special permission to work beyond normal hours and with Dr. Subha Rao's guidance and support, we embarked on a rigorous investigation into the system's behaviour. We observed that the GC system operated cyclically—performing well for 1-2 days, followed by gross misbehaviour and inconsistency. Our dedicated efforts continued for seven days, showing some improvement but falling short of the desired stability. Dr. Subha Rao, exemplifying his exceptional character, worked alongside us tirelessly, even providing our dinner from his home. Despite the challenges, he did not reject our system but suggested that we return to Baroda with some parts for rework. I candidly expressed our lack of R&D facilities in Baroda and requested permission to stay for an additional week. Generously, he agreed, allowing us to continue our work and bring the system to an acceptable level.

After a day of rest, my Engineer and I resumed our analysis of the stability issues in the system. We utilised the NCL library facilities and delved into Chromatography journals. Through our research, we discovered that the FID Detector and associated pneumatic gas control system required a thorough cleaning of all components in an ultrasonic bath using specific chemicals. The parts were then heated to a specific temperature and flushed with pure Nitrogen gas for 3-4 hours to remove any residuals from the entire system, including pneumatic and detector parts.

NCL proved to be a crucial ally in our journey to resolve the stability issues with FID system. Equipped with an ultrasonic bath and all the necessary chemicals for cleaning, NCL provided us with the ideal environment for the required maintenance. Taking a systematic approach, we carefully dismantled FID Detector and certain tubing connecting the detector. After a meticulous cleaning and drying process, we reassembled the entire system, allowing it to run overnight for gas flushing without igniting the flame. The following morning, we eagerly checked all the parameters, ensuring proper flow and then ignited the flame. To our delight, the system became stable, yielding the expected positive results. The sense of achievement was shared among all of us, including Dr. Subha Rao and his dedicated laboratory staff. The realisation that we had successfully developed the technology for the FID system filled us with immense pride and satisfaction. Credit for this achievement goes to Dr. Subha Rao, who not only played a crucial role as part of our team but also served as the Head of the department. His commitment was evident in the 10-12 days he spent with us, generously providing dinner and displaying excellent cooperation. The collaborative effort with Dr. Subha Rao and his department proved indispensable and without their support, it would have been nearly impossible to perfect the FID system in such a short time frame. We extend our heartfelt gratitude to Mrs. Subha Rao and Dr. Subha Rao for their invaluable assistance, love and co-operation.

This chapter in our journey will be eternally remembered as a testament to the spirit of collaboration and shared success as long as Chromatography and Instruments Company (CIC) exists.

Procurement of Essentiality Certificate (EC) and Import Licence

As mentioned earlier, several key components and chemicals needed for our systems had to be imported from the UK and the USA to ensure the comparability of our products with foreign brands. In the early days of our company, I personally travelled abroad to purchase these parts and brought them back as personal baggage, clearing customs at Delhi Airport with the assistance of Mr. Bhishan Kohli. This method allowed production to continue on a small-scale. To finance the purchase of these components, my brother, sister and Patel's family members supported us by making payments for the parts in the UK and the USA. However, a more permanent solution was needed and that involved obtaining an import licence from the Ministry of Commerce and Industry, Government of India, with its state office in Ahmedabad.

I visited Ministry's office in Ahmedabad to obtain the application form, but I was advised to go to the Director of Industries office in Baroda, where the application will be scrutinised. I went to General Manager's (G.M.) office at Kothi, Char Rasta, Vadodara, where Mr. Jaiswal, the G.M., who had close ties to the Chief Minister of

Gujarat, Mr. Chiman Bhai Patel, was In-charge. After meeting with Mr. Jaiswal, I received the application form for an import licence. Finding the form very complex, I sought help from a private Liaison office on Main Tower Road, as suggested by Mr. Jaiswal.

The Liaison officer informed me that, before becoming eligible for the import licence, I needed an Essentiality Certificate (EC) from the Director of Industries, Gujarat. He explained that obtaining the EC was challenging, involving an approved production plan, factory inspection and more. The officer also mentioned the high demand for import licences, with few people successfully obtaining them. He offered to assist me in acquiring the EC and import licence, requiring an advance payment of Rs. 20,000 or 10% of the approved EC value and of the import licence.

I accepted the offer and began the process. The Liaison officer guided me through the necessary steps, including inspection by the Industrial department and completing the import licence application. After submitting the application, I faced challenges with the GM's office, where Mr. Jaiswal insisted on a complete and flawless form. Despite attempts to meet

Mr. Jaiswal, I faced several obstacles that led to frustration. Eventually, I managed to confront Mr. Jaiswal and express my dissatisfaction with the treatment I received. The incident escalated and I confronted him physically, expressing my discontent. Subsequently, I left his office without interference and returned to my factory.

I attempted to contact Mr. Shivaganam, Chief Secretary of Gujarat, but he was unavailable. I developed aquaintances with Mr.Shivaganam during his visit to the University of Wales during my Ph.D. tenure at University of Wales, UK. His secretary advised me to come the next day at 11 A.M. The following day, I met with Mr. Shivaganam at his office and sought his assistance in securing a bank loan of Rs. 20,000 to facilitate the speed up of the process of completing the documents for submitting to the concerned department. To obtain the Essentiality Certificate, Mr. Shivaganam, upon hearing my request, asked for a detailed account of my dealings with the consultant. After understanding the situation, he instructed me to go to the concerned officer's office at 11 A.M. in Baroda, where he would intervene in my presence.

I reached the concerned officer's office again at 10 A.M. and waited for his arrival. When he entered his office at 10:30 A.M., he proceeded without acknowledging me. At 10:45 A.M., I entered his room and this time, the peon did not stop me. I informed the officer that Mr. Shivaganam had instructed me to be present in his office at 11 A.M. At exactly 11 A.M., a phone call interrupted us, with the officer visibly nervous during the call. Although I couldn't hear Mr. Shivaganam's side of the conversation, the office informed me afterwards that the call was from Mr. Shivaganam. He instructed me to return to my factory, assuring me that someone would visit with the necessary forms to assist its completion. The EC would be granted within 10-15 days. The following day, the designated agent arrived at our factory and we completed all the required formalities. True to Mr. Shivaganam's assurance, the officer himself visited our factory within 15 days, presenting the original EC certificate. Later, he mentioned his connection to the Chief Minister and offered further assistance, if needed. This marked the unseemly episode regarding the EC approval. We applied for an import licence of Rs. 1,00,000 only, given the exorbitant and economically unviable customs duties, leaving us with other alternatives to procure the raw material from Bombay's market.

This is how we started our production of GCs in our company in Baroda.

Purchase of know-how for Recorder from National Chemical Laboratory, Pune

Our journey with the TCD based GC began with an initial purchase order from BHU, Varanasi. This comprehensive order included a complete system, along with a Potentiometric Strip Chart Recorder, emphasising the crucial role of the recording device in the instrument's functionality. Upon receiving permission from the indenter, we transported our GC to BHU and successfully installed it with their Potentiometric Strip Chart Recorder. The GC seamlessly integrated with their recorder, marking the successful operation of the first Indian-made TCD-GC. Following this, we commenced the analysis of their gas mixture samples, impressing BHU with the GC's performance and leading to a request for a 4-5 days training session for their staff.

Once the expected results were achieved, I advised all concerned individuals to operate the equipment as per the instruction manual provided. Within a couple of days, they became proficient in using the system independently. Emphasising the simplicity of the GC operation,

I recommended confidence both in oneself and in the instrument. At the request of the Head of Department, we left the GC in their laboratory as part of their purchase order.

Regarding the recorder, recognising that it was not manufactured domestically, I arranged with Oxford Instruments of Cambridge, UK, to have their range of recorders assembled and manufactured. After completing the necessary paperwork, I applied to the Government of India for a joint venture with Oxford Instruments. However, permission for a joint venture for recorders was denied as it had already been developed by the NCL in Pune. Subsequently, we visited NCL and signed an agreement on a royalty basis to obtain the design and drawings of the recorder.

Following NCL's design, we fabricated a prototype recorder with the assistance of Mr. Bakre of NCL. Commuting between Baroda and Pune, we ensured the recorder's functionality and verified all parameters. However, upon coupling it with our GC in Varanasi, we encountered issues. Despite modifications suggested by Mr. Bakre, the recorder still failed to function. Exploring further, we discovered Mr. Bakre's interest in his privately manufactured recorders and negotiated an agreement with him. An order of five units was placed on him. These recorders were supplied to us, but they still faced functionality issues when tested with GC systems at other Universities. Despite attempts to rectify the issues, including shielding the input transformer, the recorder remained non-functional, posing a significant challenge.

Upon returning to NCL, I confronted Mr. Bakre regarding the malfunctioning of recorders. Despite his claims that the recorder was operational in his laboratory, I was frustrated and ended up slapping him. This altercation escalated into a scuffle, leading to my arrest on charges of attacking a Government officer on duty. NCL officials collaborated with the police in filing a complaint against me, adding to the gravity of the situation. I also lodged a complaint against NCL. Around two hours later, representatives from NCL approached me and requested the withdrawal of my complaint, as they were willing to withdraw theirs as well. Initially, I refused, insisting on a refund and compensation for the business loss incurred. However, the Director of NCL intervened, urging me to withdraw my complaint. Despite my initial resistance, Mr. Lale, an Administrative Officer at NCL, persuaded me by expressing his support and holding my feet as a sign of humility. In consideration of our friendship and Mr. Lale's assurance of backing from the Director, I relented and agreed to withdraw the complaint.

The following day, I attempted to meet the Director, NCL but was denied entry by security due to the lack of a prior request for my visit. It became apparent that I had been barred from NCL premises. Despite this, no further communication was received from NCL and our business dealings with the laboratory ceased. Notably, the Director had family ties to Central Minister Mr. H.R. Gokhale during that period and the political connections between Bakre, the Director and the Central Minister likely influenced the outcome of the situation.

This incident prompted us to procure imported recorders temporarily to complete our GC set-up. After concerted efforts, we successfully resolved the issues and our recorder began functioning seamlessly with our GCs. Subsequently, with the deployment and refinement of our recorder, several Indian companies began manufacturing recorders within the country, marking a significant development in the Industry.

Purchase of know-how for Electron Capture Detector from Bhabha Atomic Research Centre

In 1970s, there was a significant surge in demand for GCs equipped with advanced detectors such as TCD, FID and Electron Capture Detector (ECD). The ECD, specifically tailored for detecting pesticides, insecticides and agricultural chemicals, represented cutting-edge technology held by the Bhabha Atomic Research Centre (BARC) in Mumbai. Obtaining this technology from BARC included access to the detector's design. With the guidance of Dr. Iyer from BARC's Chemistry Division, we successfully manufactured an ECD. Notably, ECDs involve the utilisation of a low-intensity radioactive source, Tritium, exclusively supplied by BARC and subject to stringent accountability measures. Once depleted, the radioactive source needed to be returned to BARC authorities for safe disposal.

Despite our efforts, challenges emerged regarding the performance of the ECDs in practical applications. Customers expressed dissatisfaction primarily due to contamination of the source by impurities present in the samples being analysed. Additionally, the GC system required a significant amount of time to flush the ECD and eliminate impurities settled on the source. The detector had an upper-temperature limit of 200 degrees Celsius, with conditioning performed at a maximum of 190 degrees Celsius. These issues resulted in user dissatisfaction and hesitancy in adopting the technology.

In response to these challenges, we conducted visits to various Industries and Research Institutes utilising ECDs. Industry experts highlighted the importance of using Nickel-63 (Ni^{63}) as a radioactive source, capable of withstanding higher temperatures, up to 350 degrees Celsius. They emphasised that Tritium radioactive sources, which we were utilising, were suitable only for gas analysis, not for liquid applications. However, due to the unavailability of Ni^{63} sources in India and challenges in obtaining licences for importing radioactive sources, we faced obstacles in addressing these concerns. Consequently, we made the decision to cease the manufacturing of ECDs.

Presently, we offer an alternative to ECDs with a non-radioactive source. We have supplied numerous GCs to BARC, featuring non-radioactive detectors suitable for similar applications, ensuring compliance with safety regulations and meeting the requirements of our customers. We continue to import this detector from VICI Valco, Switzerland and VICI USA, along with their associated electronics, as developing this detector in-house is not currently feasible due to relatively low demand.

Author's Books on Chromatography

Following the establishment of our company, which focused on Chromatography Instrumentation in 1972, I began actively marketing our products from 1974 onwards. During the seventies, GCs were regarded as highly advanced electronic instruments, incorporating a significant blend of Chemistry and Electronics. Primarily utilised by Chemists, Metallurgists and Chemical Engineers, these instruments found extensive applications in analytical laboratories and the process industries. I encountered significant challenges when attempting to explain the concept of Chromatography to individuals in the aforementioned technical categories, as many of them lacked awareness of Chromatography even up to M.Sc. level. Recognising this gap in understanding, I made the decision to write a book on Chromatography specifically tailored for beginners, Chemists, Engineers and users of GC.

First Book

My aim was to make it clearer and easier to understand the imaginary view that Chromatography was a highly sophisticated and difficult instrument **to handle and use for their day-to-day applications.** In 1988, I authored the "Handbook on Chromatography for Chemists and Engineers," with the intention of providing a comprehensive resource that would educate novices and users of Chromatography alike. This handbook proved to be immensely beneficial in simplifying the concepts associated with Chromatography, thereby enabling individuals from diverse technical backgrounds to grasp its principles and applications more effectively.

Second Book

In December 1978, I had the opportunity to present two significant chapters at the Symposium and Workshop on "Chromatography of Polymers, Petroleum and Petrochemicals," held at the Indian Association for the Cultivation of Science in Calcutta. This event served as a platform to discuss and exchange insights on chromatographic techniques as they relate to polymers, petroleum and petrochemicals.

The symposium was curated by **Dr. Sukumar Maiti, Head of the Materials Science Centre at the IIT, Kharagpur.** My contributions to this symposium highlighted the application of Chromatography in the analysis and characterisation of Polymers, Petroleum and Petrochemicals. These chapters aimed to elucidate the role of chromatographic methods in addressing the unique challenges posed by these complex materials, offering valuable insights into their composition, properties and behaviour.

This endeavour underscored my commitment in advancing the understanding and utilisation of Chromatography across diverse fields of Science and Industry. By sharing my expertise and research findings at such prestigious gatherings, I aimed to contribute to the broader scientific community and facilitate advancements in analytical techniques and methodologies.

Third Book

In 1989, Dr. N.A. Emanuel, the R&D Manager at the Research Centre of CIC and I collaborated to compile a book titled "Atlas of Chromatography." This collaborative effort aimed to create a comprehensive resource that would serve as a guide and reference for professionals and enthusiasts in the field of Chromatography.

The **"Atlas of Chromatography"** sought to provide a visual and informative overview of various chromatographic techniques, methodologies and applications. Through detailed illustrations, diagrams and explanatory text, the book aims to demystify Chromatography and its diverse applications across different industries and scientific disciplines.

Our goal in compiling this Atlas was to bridge the gap between theory and practice, offering practical insights and visual representations of chromatographic processes and analyses. By presenting a wide range of chromatographic methods and their real-world applications, we aimed to equip readers with the knowledge and tools needed to apply Chromatography effectively in their respective fields.

The collaborative effort between **Dr. Emanuel** and myself brought together our expertise and experiences in Chromatography, resulting in a valuable resource that could benefit Researchers, Scientists, Educators and Students alike. The "Atlas of Chromatography" represented our commitment in advancing the understanding and **utilisation of Chromatography as a powerful analytical tool in scientific research and industrial applications.**

Summary

Section 6: Dreams Now Converted into Reality

Major incidents:

1. Expansion of my family – welcoming Gaurav and Amar in our lives.
2. Application of the 'MAKE IN INDIA' ethos in our lives. Commencement of construction work at the company and initiation of the manufacturing process for Gas Chromatographs (GC).
3. Relocating to 'Parishram.'
4. Procurement of Essentiality Certificate (EC) and Import Licence and writing books on Chromatography – for beginners, Chemists, Engineers and users of GC.

Learning:

1. The dream to perform and deliver at one's homeland, in itself, is the biggest motivation one can ever have.
2. The learning and unlearning during the transitions while travelling between two cities,

helped in understanding various cultures and the cultural ethics being followed while setting up of the business.

3. There is always an opportunity cost involved when you want to make your dream – A reality.

Chapter defining quote:

"It is overwhelming to see that the fruits of the efforts put in are more than what has been asked for. Hence, the initiative of scripting it down as a successful journey to help others achieve their dreams and setting up an example is indeed a profound experience and thus, there is a need to share the journey with others who are in search of such light in their dark phases."

Section 7
The Art of Asset Building

"If there is any heaven, it is on earth and on earth, it is in "Parishram," of the Doctor & Doctor Building."

Part I: Inception of Industry: Chromatography & Instruments Co. Pvt. Ltd

After a mutual agreement between Mr. Shrish Patel and I, we decided to establish a private limited company that would eventually assume control of the partnership company. The long-term plan involved transitioning to a public limited company to facilitate expansion into a broader range of products and other activities in the instrumentation sector.

The company was formally registered with the Registrar of Companies in Ahmedabad, featuring an authorised share capital of Rs. 35 Lakhs, divided into Rs. 3.5 Lakhs equity shares of Rs. 10 each. Both Mr. Patel and I assumed directorship roles in CIC Pvt. Ltd. effective from December 5th, 1975. However, minimal activity occurred in the private limited company until Mr. Patel's retirement in October 1980. During this period, the company existed only on paper and remained dormant until 1982. Following my takeover of the partnership company, I decided to construct a four-story building, with each floor encompassing approximately 4200 sq. ft. The building featured independent stairs and was situated on a separate plot, designated as plot no. 121. Subsequently, CIC continued to occupy plot no. 122. Both entities operated independently and occupied separate plots. The building's construction plan was approved towards the end of 1982 and construction commenced in 1983, concluding with the issuance of the completion certificate in 1984. Since then, CIC and CIC Pvt. Ltd. have occupied their respective independent buildings.

After the building's completion, we leased it to ONGC field parties returning from the field during the monsoon period. This arrangement continued for several years until ONGC vacated the premises. Subsequently, the building was leased to M/s. Star Machinery Limited of Bombay. After a few years, Star Machinery relocated to their own building in GIDC and our building became available again. Various companies occupied and later vacated the space based on their specific requirements. Eventually, CIC Pvt. Ltd. began utilising the building for its own operations.

As of today, we are using a few floors for manufacturing as well as trading. For the later, we require a good amount of space to accommodate the materials that are either imported from GE UK or bought directly from GE Bangalore. Also, two Microwave towers are located in our premises:

1. One Mobile Tower – Roof Top w.e.f. 01-08-2009
2. One Mobile Tower – on ground w.e.f. 05-10-2009

Each of the four companies is currently contributing a good amount of monthly rent, illustrating the successful realisation of my vision, strategic planning and effective implementation. This achievement stands in stark contrast to the challenges faced by Mr. Shrish Patel, who lacked the necessary criteria for future growth and financial support. Currently, CIC Pvt. Ltd. operates as a trading company and holds the distributorship of General Electric (GE) Company, UK. A visual representation of the company's premises is shown as under. Apart from our rental income from the buildings, our trading business with General Electric has increased manifolds.

Photograph of CIC Pvt. Ltd

Part II: Genesis of Greatness: The Construction of the Dr. & Dr. Buildings

Construction of Doctor & Doctor Building No. 1

Our plan for a three-story building was sanctioned and we obtained the plinth check certificate on February 12, 1981 and the Completion Certificate on October 29, 1995. I conceptualised the architectural design for the building, allocating the ground floor for the factory, the second floor for office space and the third floor for senior staff working within the company. This large building is now recognised as the Doctor & Doctor Building.

The construction of this building experienced a delay because, concurrently, I initiated the construction of a second building mirroring the first, complete with a common staircase and provision for a lift. I aimed to obtain the Completion Certificate simultaneously for both structures, as Government taxes commence from the date of acquiring the Completion Certificate. The strategic planning was aimed at leasing out both buildings together to potential multinational tenants. This strategic decision materialised, as both buildings were eventually leased out to Protect Circuit Breaker Limited in Gujarat.

Construction of Doctor & Doctor Building No. 2

I constructed a second three-story building adjacent to the first one, featuring a shared staircase and four toilets on each floor. The plan for this building was approved in 1983 and the Plinth Check Certificate (PCC) was issued by the Baroda Municipality Corporation (BMC) on June 1, 1984. The construction was completed and the Completion Certificate was obtained on January 16, 1985. Following this, I decided to transfer ownership of this unfinished building. Initially, after reaching the plinth level of this building, I sold the unconstructed portion up to the plinth level to my wife. We obtained the PCC from BMC. Construction commenced in 1983 and concluded in 1985. A sale deed was executed at the Registrar's office in Kothi building, Baroda. Dr. (Mrs.) Kiran Shingari formed her proprietary company under the name Kiran Associates, which secured electrical and water connections and also paid Municipal taxes. In 1985, after obtaining the Completion Certificate and securing all necessary facilities like electrical connection, water connection, drainage connection, etc., the building was ready for use.

Subsequently, the building was leased out to Protect Circuit Breaker Limited, with both floors generating substantial revenue, providing me with the financial strength to take risks for further expansion.

Building 1 **Building 2**

After fully completing the Doctor and Doctor buildings, my eldest son Gaurav got married to Lovely Sethi and subsequently, they were blessed with two beautiful daughters – Mallika and Shubhangini. After Gaurav's marriage, Amar married Poonam Mehra and they were blessed with two wonderful children – a son named Arya and a daughter named Anoushkaa. Subsequently, my family grew and my heart grew along with it, as evident by the pictures below.

Gaurav's Marriage and Family

Photograph of Amar's Marriage

All four grandchildren were born in the Dr. and Dr. building:

As of now, both industrial buildings, Doctor & Doctor and Kiran Associates, have been leased out to M/s. Omgene Life Sciences Private Limited for the past five years. Doctor & Doctor Building No. 1 generates a good amount of monthly rent and contributes a good amount of revenue after paying Income Tax in the 35.1% range, including all cess and surcharge.

Happy Family of Four

Part III: Constructing Comfort: CIC Guest House "Parishram"

Construction of "Parishram": The CIC Guest House

The construction of Chromatography and Instrument Company's Guest House on an industrial plot in GIDC Makarpura posed a unique challenge. In the early months of 1979, however, after meeting the top officers of GIDC in Baroda and also of BMC, I successfully persuaded GIDC and BMC authorities by emphasising our potential joint venture with a UK-based company. The plan for the company's Guest House was approved and we began construction accordingly. At the time, my family and I were residing in a B-type quarter in the GIDC colony and desired a more suitable accommodation to accommodate our foreign visitors as well as Indian buyers. We served Government organisations and highly qualified users and needed proper accommodation for training purposes and for the visiting Officers and Scientists. The revised plan was approved as a "Guest House" by both GIDC and BMC. The BMC issued the PCC on August 12, 1990. Subsequently, the Completion Certificate was granted on August 26, 1991, by Deputy Town Development Officer of BMC. However, an issue arose when the officer refused to issue the

Completion Certificate, a crucial document for obtaining water supply, an independent electric meter and a drainage connection.

CIC Guest House

Despite the confrontation, within a month, a new Deputy Town Development Officer issued the Completion Certificate. With this document, we finally obtained the necessary facilities and services, which had been withheld during the conflict with the previous officer. We started the use of our Guest House “Parishram,” part of the Doctor & Doctor plots, in the middle of 1992. Since then, we have been accommodating our foreign as well as Indian guests who come to us for inspection, training, demonstrations, etc.

Summary

Section 7: The Art of Asset Building

Major incidents:

1. Construction of Chromatography & Instruments Co. Pvt. Ltd premises, which are the backbone of our industrial efforts.
2. Construction of the Dr. & Dr. Buildings, our pride and joy.
3. Construction of the CIC Guest House for Foreign dignitaries, Government of India officials and training and demonstration personnel when they visit the industry.

Learning:

1. Invest smartly in asset building early on in the setting up of an industry without undue hesitancy. A well-thought-out plan in real estate can help the industry flourish.
2. Keep the documentation clear for all stages of construction. One should clearly know the important dates and events in his or her mind.

3. Never fear corrupt officials when embarking on such a huge and costly endeavour. If done with proper and honest intention, the Nature will guarantee your success.

Chapter defining quote:

"If there is any heaven, it is on earth and on earth, it is in "Parishram," of the Dr. & Dr. Building."

Section 8
The Absolute Cost of Success and Ambition

"Beware of the unknown foes (Agyaat Shatru)."

Part I: The Toll of a Partner's Betrayal

The Battlefield is set: Introducing the Partners and their Families

Chromatography and Instruments Company had two partners: Mr. Shrish Patel and myself. I extended an invitation to Mr. Patel to join me as a partner in the venture I began and he accepted. Mr. Patel had completed his M.Sc. in Electrical Engineering simultaneously as I completed my Ph.D. in Chemical Engineering from the University of Wales. I believe it is prudent to provide details about both partners involved and their respective families to give a holistic understanding of the situation. It is outlined below:

Dr. M.K. Shingari

Possessing a Ph.D., I have around two years of experience in industries in the UK and an additional year of experience in India. Described by my associates and friends as disciplined, hard-working, quick-thinking, short-tempered and adept at making rapid decisions, I am known for my ability to work efficiently and extract the best from those assigned to assist me. People who know me well note that I have a dominant personality and once a decision is made, it is final, with no room for compromise or a change of mind. While considered kind-hearted, I am often described as blunt in speech, a characteristic noted by both colleagues and professors in College and University. I got married in November 1972, after the formation of the company in India. After marriage, my wife and in-laws echoed similar sentiments about my personality, emphasising my independent views or decisions and determination.

Mr. Shrish Patel

Holding an M.Sc. degree, Mr. Shrish Patel was married to Saryu Patel, with no children at the time of the company's formation. His father migrated from South Africa to India, while the rest of his family, including brothers and sisters, relocated to the UK. Mr. Patel and his family held British citizenship. Saryu's family comprised four sisters and one brother, all of whom migrated to India from South Africa. Mr. Shrish Patel was characterised as a simple person with a strong family background, though his personality was considered less assertive compared to mine. He demonstrated average discipline and displayed an ability to connect well with the local Gujarati community, but he faced challenges in understanding individuals from other communities. His decision-making skills were deemed poor and he often displayed indecisiveness. He was known for his slow pace, which sometimes influenced those working under him. However, a commendable aspect of his character was his honesty.

Mr. Patel's wife, Mrs. Saryu Ben, held a B.A. degree and was known for her assertiveness, reminiscent of her own mother. Shrish Patel was considered fully henpecked, indicating a significant influence from his wife. Saryu Ben expressed deep admiration for my personality, clothing and communication skills, often remarking, "Mahender Bhai can captivate anyone; he could put someone in a bottle." She consistently urged Shrish to learn from my way of living and acting. In my personal opinion, this admiration may have been rooted in her own feelings of inferiority.

Shrish Patel was responsible for overseeing production, stores, accounts and factory management, while my focus was on marketing, involving approximately 20 days of travel per month for GC installations and related tasks. Upon returning from my tours, I frequently found a crowd of people waiting outside the office for various payment-related matters. These discussions and arguments were affecting the efficiency of our office and consuming a significant amount of Shrish's time. Sharing the office with Shrish, I proposed that I take over the responsibility of handling stores and accounts, allowing him to concentrate on production and product improvement. Despite some reluctance, he agreed to the arrangement.

Taking charge of the pending bills from subcontractors, I scrutinised each one and instructed our storekeeper, who happened to be Patel, to arrange a meeting with all the vendors on a single day. I committed to addressing their concerns and resolving payment issues. Almost all the vendors with outstanding bills attended the meeting and I started discussing each case individually. During the examination of their bills, it became apparent that the non-payment was due to the fact that part of the supplied material did not meet specifications and was rejected, with an average rejection rate ranging from 5% to 20%.

I called vendors into my office, discussed the rejected materials and established timelines for the replacement of defective items. Following their adherence to the agreed-upon schedules, I released payments for items meeting our specifications, deducting only the amount corresponding to the rejected items.

This approach left all the vendors satisfied and they started offering discounts of 3-5% for prompt payments. While the vendors were content with the streamlined process, my partner was not pleased because the line of people outside our office disappeared, allowing us to focus on our work without interruptions. This situation serves as a vivid illustration of the different working styles of the two partners.

Both our families resided in one-room apartments provided by the company. My apartment boasted a front and side garden, reflecting my passion for nature and gardening. In contrast, Shrish Bhai showed little interest in these activities. I enjoyed having drinks, a preference not shared by Shrish Bhai, who was a teetotaler. I would have a peg with my senior staff, working with me until late at night during our initial days. It became routine for everyone to share a peg at my home before heading to their respective houses. Shrish and Saryu spent most of their time with her in-laws and dined there. Due to my regular gatherings, I gained popularity in the colony, while Shrish Patel remained relatively unknown, often staying with his in-laws in a very posh area.

It's worth noting that I find it challenging to connect with individuals who are considered henpecked husbands. All my friends and my children come from families where the man plays a dominant role. After two years in the GIDC colony, Shrish Patel moved to a rented house in Manjalpur, where we continued to reside.

Storm Clouds Gather: Mr. Patel goes to the US and the UK.

Our financial year 1979 – 1980 proved to be highly profitable, prompting us to consider improvements in our product line and expansion, including seeking foreign agencies. In a collaborative decision, I suggested to Shrish Patel that he should visit the USA first to negotiate with our raw material supplier and explore potential discounts. Being the senior partner, I gave him the initial opportunity. Both Mr. Patel and his wife were excited about their 5 to 6-week trip to the USA, with plans to spend an additional week in England to meet family members.

Mr. Patel, accompanied by his wife, departed for the USA in the first week of August 1980 and returned to Baroda during the third week of September. However, upon his return, he refrained from coming to the factory for about a week, citing health concerns and doctor's advice for complete rest. Toward the end of September, he gradually resumed his visits to the factory. Upon his return, he found twenty GCs meticulously packed in cardboard boxes and ready for dispatch. He discussed the packed instruments with the Engineers and briefly reviewed the accounts with the accountant. Although he visited the factory for a short period, he did not express enthusiasm or acknowledge the significant progress made by the company during his absence.

Around the end of September, when Mr. Patel visited the factory briefly, I was at the R&D Centre of IPCL. Later, during my visit to his house, I inquired about the tour report, expecting an update on the business and expenses incurred during his USA trip. To my surprise, he mentioned that he would submit the tour report and expenses bill in 3 – 4 days. It was unexpected that after returning from such a crucial visit, he did not resume regular attendance at the company as he did before he left. Throughout his interactions, he maintained serious outward behaviour, not expressing joy or acknowledgement of the company's achievements during his absence. The company had successfully manufactured and stored twenty gas GCs, a significant accomplishment that could alleviate concerns about production when focusing on marketing.

During a casual evening with our auditor, Mr. Ishwar Bhai Haribhakti, at our house, the discussion turned to Shrish's USA visit and the current state of business. I mentioned that Shrish had not provided the tour report and expenses bill and he wasn't attending the factory regularly after returning, citing health reasons. Mr. Haribhakti, after some general discussion, suddenly inquired about any tensions or issues between Shrish Patel and myself. Both Kiran and I dismissed any such concerns, stating that everything was normal. However, Mr. Haribhakti, in a mysterious manner, warned me to be cautious of unknown enemies (*Aghyat Shatru*), offering no further explanation. Despite my inquiries, he simply advised me to be careful and then left for his house.

On 5th October, we hosted a dinner party at our residence in the GIDC colony, celebrating my son Gaurav's birthday. The gathering included various guests, including Mr. Haribhakti and Shrish Patel. Patel, Saryu and their daughter left the party early, claiming that they needed to visit his father-in-law in the hospital. After Patel's departure, Mr. Haribhakti approached me, revealing that Patel seemed unhappy and had scheduled an appointment with him for the 7th of October at 11 A.M. Mr. Haribhakti suggested that I attend the meeting alone in his office so he could hear Patel's concerns in my presence and gather my views.

Curiously, he also inquired about the amount of money I had in the bank. I explained that I had recently purchased the Fatehgunj office for Rs. 8 Lakhs through his office, leaving no significant funds in the bank. He then advised me to reach out to my friends in Baroda in case of an emergency and inquire if they would be willing to help. An intuitive feeling hinted that something unusual was happening, especially since I had noticed Mr. Patel's frequent absence from the factory, making brief visits to meet the staff before leaving.

On 6th October, the following morning, Kiran and I left home at 7 A.M. to visit Ishwar Bhai Haribhakti's house. We approached him, requesting information on the developments within the company and specifically inquired about Shrish Bhai's frequent visits to his office. This revelation came from our friend Mr. Bhagwat, who had been handling our personal Income Tax returns along with the company's Income Tax returns. Our relationship with Mr. Bhagwat has always been and still is, one of the strongest friendships.

Ishwar Bhai conveyed to me that Shrish was extremely dissatisfied with my management style and a significant portion of the staff felt intimidated by my approach. He highlighted that I had recently terminated several individuals from the company, including my own brother, Mr. Surinder Shingari. This created discomfort for Shrish. Ishwar Bhai urged me to speculate on what might have upset Shrish and strained our working relationship.

After careful consideration, I identified two recent changes that might have contributed to Shrish's unease. First, the decision to shift the responsibility of stores and accounts from Shrish to myself and second, the rapid production of twenty GCs in a short timeframe, a task that would have typically taken him six months. Additionally, I terminated slow and inefficient staff, emphasising my preference for working with efficient and fast-paced individuals.

While I believed these changes were beneficial for the company's profitability, Mr. Haribhakti sensed that they could be the reasons behind Shrish's desire to separate from the partnership. During our conversation, I told Ishwar Bhai that I had purchased a hall of 5,500 sq ft. at Eagle Apartments, Fatehgaunj and exhausted all my savings. On his advice and the help of his office, this deal had been concluded. The promoter of Eagle Apartments, Mr. Kalumal, had promised to hand over the entire floor consisting of four flats as per plan within two months. Keeping this in mind, we contacted the LIC Head Office in Mumbai, headed by Kiran's cousin, Mr. Prithvi Raj Singh. On Mrs. Singh's advice, we were negotiating with LIC to take the hall to be used as their branch office in that area and eventually, LIC agreed and took it on a lease, staying there for 20 years. Ishwar Bhai also speculated that jealousy from Saryu Ben, Shrish's wife, might have played a role in pressurising Shrish to seek separation. Ishwar bhai advised that I speak to Shrish Bhai's father at Vallabh Vidyanagar as well as his father-in-law, who lived in Alkapuri.

I visited V.V. Nagar and met Shrish's father, Shri Bhailal Bhai Patel and explained what was happening after his son's arrival from the US. His response was that he, his wife, his son, who was a doctor and his son's wife, all of whom came for the holidays in India, also strongly advised Shrish not to make such a blunder. But he did not listen to them and as a result, they were very apologetic. I made an attempt to contact his in-laws in Alkapuri as well. Everybody said that he was making a big mistake by breaking the partnership.

Mr. Haribhakti also expressed regret, stating that he could have helped me if I hadn't invested in such a substantial piece of land. He emphasised that funds were running low. Luckily, I had a network of friends who could potentially help me secure the necessary finances.

Those who do not Bend Break: The Partnership Dissolves and CIC is Auctioned

On 6th October 1980, I set out with Kiran on my scooter at 7 A.M. to meet Mr. V. Charandas, the Executive Director of the Gujarat State Fertiliser Corporation. I shared the concerns Ishwar Bhai conveyed with him. Mr. Charandas vehemently advised against parting with the company, emphasising that it was my creation and should remain with me. He also assured me of his support if needed. Following our discussion, Mr. and Mrs. Charandas invited us for breakfast and later, we proceeded to the Chemical Centre, Baroda's largest dealer in Laboratory Chemicals, to meet its senior partner, Mr. Rashik Bhai Shah. We explained the situation to him and received further endorsement of Mr. Charandas' advice.

Regarding financial help, Mr. Shah offered to provide his wife's ornaments as collateral for a loan, but I declined, stating that I couldn't resort to such measures for the sake of business. As we were leaving, he handed me a photograph of Vaishnodevi Mataji, suggesting I keep it in my briefcase for good luck during discussions with my partner. I reached out to all my friends in Baroda and the majority responded positively.

On 7th October, I arrived at Mr. Haribhakti's office at 11 A.M. Mr. Patel was late, offering an apology, which delayed the start of our meeting. During this time, I consulted Mr. Bhagwat, Ishwar Bhai's partner and received unanimous support. The meeting commenced at twelve noon, involving Ishwar Bhai, Bachu Bhai, Shrish Patel and myself.

Ishwar Bhai inquired if I had any problems with Shrish Bhai, to which I replied in the negative, expressing satisfaction with my partner. Ishwar Bhai posed the same question to Shrish Patel, who stated his desire to exit the company and proposed either that I take over or hand the company to him. Shrish Patel suggested that the buyer should pay 50% of the company's share value to the existing partner. When Ishwar Bhai asked me if this proposal was acceptable, I disagreed and suggested a joint evaluation of the company's assets after taking stock of the finished goods, unfinished goods and raw materials. Shrish Patel proposed auctioning the company, agreeing that the highest bidder should acquire it. I supported this idea but urged Ishwar Bhai to settle the terms and conditions for the auction first. As our discussion unfolded, someone arrived and handed each of us a separate letter in a cover, totalling three letters for the three individuals involved.

We opened the letter and saw the contents.

After reading the letter, I said, "Shrish Bhai, you've drafted this and you are a real bastard. Now, I will not allow you to take the company." After this, I told Ishwar Bhai to settle the conditions, which are as follows:

1. The company auction will take place now.
2. Whosoever pays more will take over the company.
3. 50% of the auction value has to be paid to the outgoing partner today itself.
4. The cheque is to be given in the presence of all the people present.
5. If the cheque is not honoured, the other partner will make the payment as per his offered value.
6. No extension shall be given.

Both partners agreed and signed the terms and conditions discussed in the presence of Ishwar Bhai Haribhakti, who countersigned the documents. Since I was very angry, my first offer was Rs. 5 Lakhs. Shrish Patel offered

Rs. 5.25 Lakhs and I offered Rs. 5.75 Lakhs. Patel raised his offer to Rs. 6 Lakhs until we reached up to Rs. 8 Lakhs. I had made up my mind not to give my company to Patel at any cost because of the letter he had given during the auction. I kept on repeating, “Patel, now you cannot have the company.”

Patel’s last offer was Rs. 8 Lakhs and my counteroffer was Rs. 10 Lakhs. Everybody in the meeting was perplexed by my jump of Rs. 2 Lakhs. I felt that they could see the anger on my face and thought that I had lost my mind. “How can Shingari pay Rs. 5 Lakhs immediately when his bank balance is zero?” they thought. I am sure that Ishwar Bhai and Shrish Patel both knew that I did not have the money as all my savings had been used to purchase the new office building in Fatehgunj. They were sure that I would not be able to make the payment that day. Patel stopped at this level and said he would accept Rs. 5 Lakhs and transfer his share to me. Haribhakti and Company started preparing an agreement and told me to go and get the chequebook and issue a cheque of Rs. 5 Lakhs by the name of Mr. Shrish Patel for 6th October 1980. Ishwar Bhai provided his personal auto-rickshaw and instructed the driver to take me to GIDC and bring me back immediately. I went home, took my chequebook and told the driver to stop at the Bank of Baroda, which was on our way.

I met the Bank Manager, Mr. Mohit Shah and the officer, Mr. Kirit Shah and told them everything. They told me to issue the cheque and somehow delay it as long as I could so that Patel would come with the cheque after the closing time of the transaction. "We will accept the cheque and keep it with us till tomorrow afternoon; till then, you organise the money and if any problem arises, we both will help you," they assured me. They also told me that once I had given the cheque and signed the paper, I would take over the company. I handled the account and factory keys were also with me as I opened and closed the factory to ensure discipline in the company. I signed the cheque at 4 P.M. and handed it over to Ishwar Bhai to pass on to Patel, along with his letter duly signed by him in the presence of Ishwar Bhai Haribhakti in his office on 7th October at 4 P.M. After this time, I would become the sole proprietor and not a partner. As per the agreement, if the cheque bounced, Patel would pay me Rs. 5 Lakhs and become the sole proprietor.

After this Patel went to the Bank of Baroda and the bank said that the check could not be cashed as their transaction time was over and they had closed their accounts. Mr. Mohit Shah said, "You come here tomorrow after 11 A.M. and we will deposit the cheque in your account and transfer the amount equal to the cheque value which will be credited tomorrow morning, so do not worry Shrish Bhai."

I came home and went to Mr. Mohit's house and took his advice. He told me, "You are the owner of the company and can use the company's chequebook to transfer the money from the company's account to your personal accounts. You collect the money and whatever is short you issue the company's cheque for that amount. We will credit the amount in your account."

I surrendered our FDRs which were with the Bank of Baroda. I also went to all my friends and managed to arrange Rs. 3.75 Lakhs, falling short by Rs. 1.25 Lakhs. I went to the bank at 10 am and deposited all the cash and also issued a company's cheque to my account which was credited into my savings account.

As a result, the balance in my account became over Rs. 5 Lakhs. Mr. Patel came to the bank around 11:30 A.M. and deposited the cheque in his account. Kirit Bhai completed the transaction after crediting Rs. 5 Lakhs into Shrish Bhai Patel's account. My account was debited for the same amount. I informed Ishwar Bhai Haribhakti that Rs. 5 Lakhs had been credited into Shrish's account. He wanted to know how I had managed this incredible feat and I replied that it was not the right time to talk about it. Both Mr. Mohit Shah, the Manager and Mr. Kirit Shah, the officer, are still alive and they occasionally visit our factory and house.

The Hard Times Continue: Employees Depart and the Shingari Household is Besieged

All the employees of CIC and CIC Pvt. Ltd. collectively presented their grievances in the midst of the company auction at our auditor's office. Their primary concerns were directed towards my managerial capabilities and the perceived unjust decisions to terminate employees without any apparent cause. Upon the acquisition of both companies, I, as the new owner, took the decision to deny them entry into the company premises. I advised them to submit their resignations, citing their lack of confidence in me and my management.

Despite this suggestion, they adamantly refused to tender their resignations and attempted to forcibly enter the premises. In response to their persistence, I issued a warning, cautioning against the consequences of attempting forced entry. I even took the drastic step of displaying my revolver, explicitly stating that any unauthorised entry would be met with severe consequences, including potential harm. I reiterated that they were considered disloyal employees and had no place within my company. Despite these warnings, the employees revealed that a representation letter had been drafted by Mr. Shrish, who had influenced them by portraying me as a temperamental and unreliable leader. Even in light of these revelations, I remained firm in denying them access to the company and secured the premises with a lock.

Subsequently, all the employees visited the Makarpura Police Choki and filed a complaint against me, alleging that I was preventing them from entering the premises. They argued that their employment had not been terminated and as employees of the company, they should be allowed to resume work, considering their role as breadwinners for their families. Inspector Chudasama of the Makarpura police station, a close friend of Colonel Samsher Singh, former ADC of Maharaja Gaikwad, intervened in an attempt to mediate the situation. Inspector Chudasama advised the employees to contact him the next day after he had spoken to me.

To address the escalating situation, I sought the assistance of Mr. Ishwar Bhai Haribhakti and a resolution was proposed. It was agreed that the employees' salaries would be paid upon the tendering of their resignations. Mr. Haribhakti arranged for one of his accountants to be present at our residence with the necessary funds and vouchers, ensuring that the factory remained locked until all employees had signed the required documents. The following day, all the employees approached Mr. Chudasama, who informed them that I was not agreeing to their proposal. However, through persuasion, I was convinced to pay their salaries for the last month and the number of days they had worked in the company.

Despite this compromise, the employees were insistent on not resigning and instead wanted me to terminate their services. This defiance angered Inspector Chudasama, leading him to take drastic action. He slapped their leader, Mr. Kutty, as well as Mr. Chalke, the secretary and accountant of CIC and expelled them from the police station. Mr. Chudasama gave them a two-day ultimatum to come to my house and collect their salaries from the accountant provided by Ishwar Bhai Haribhakti.

The next day, five employees decided to resign and collect their salaries, leaving three – an accountant, a secretary and a worker. On the following day, the police were sent to bring the remaining three employees to the police station in a jeep. Mr. Chudasama reiterated his advice, suggesting that they resign for their own benefit and receive their full salaries. Faced with the police intervention, they eventually tendered their resignations, expressing regret for being swayed by Mr. Patel's advice.

To avoid any unwanted incidents, we kept the factory closed for the next three to four days. Upon reopening, only two individuals, my wife Kiran and I, took command of a company that my so-called partner had tried to dismantle.

We cleared all small loans taken from friends through the overdraft facility of our Bank of Baroda account. We urgently requested that Kiran's parents, to come to Baroda. Upon their arrival, Kiran's mother took the responsibility of looking after our children, Gaurav and Amar, while Prof. Vohra, Kiran and I assumed the task of running the company. Mr. Haribhakti recommended Mr. Soni as a full-time accountant and we also relocated our gardener, Mr. Gamal Singh, to the factory. With this team of five individuals, we embarked on the journey of re-building the company.

Confident in the quality of the 20 GCs manufactured under my supervision, we anticipated flourishing with sufficient funds generated from the sales of these high-quality instruments.

The Final Blow: From Dear Partners to Bitter Rivals

After two unsuccessful attempts to oust me from CIC and CIC Pvt. Ltd., Mr. Patel initiated his own venture named M/s. Sigma Instruments focuses on manufacturing similar products. He recruited all eight individuals who had been compelled to resign from Chromatography & Instruments Company. With a fully trained workforce familiar with vendors and subcontractors, he commenced production, emerging as an active competitor to my precious company. Within six months, he introduced GCs and recorders into the market cent per cent based on the CIC design, complete with marketing literature and instruction manuals that closely mirrored my own products. Driven by a vengeful motive, Mr. Patel, along with his former team, was determined to eliminate me from the market. To accomplish this objective, he employed a multi-pronged strategy, opening three fronts to undermine my business. These strategies were:

1. Reduction in price by 40-50 % from my list price.
2. Visiting all my dealers and distributors and convincing them to discontinue the distributorship of CIC, thus becoming his distributor on the pretext that he was the main production man in CIC anyway.
3. Spreading rumours that CIC is closing down because all staff, production and marketing personnel had resigned and joined his company. CIC did not even have any staff to function.

Due to the limited manpower in the company, consisting only Kiran and myself, it became impractical for us to engage in active marketing efforts. Mr. Patel took advantage of this situation and advised some customers who were acquainted with him to contact me for the servicing of their GCs, stating that the supplied instruments were not functioning properly and required an immediate servicing. They promised that they would pay the service charges, whatever these may be. While it was indeed challenging for me to attend these service calls, my primary focus was on securing orders, ensuring the supply and installation of instruments and promptly receiving payments to maintain a smooth financial operation.

Exploiting the circumstances, Mr. Patel began spreading rumours that I intended to return to the UK. I was already in the UK and exploring job opportunities for myself; he claimed that I had already visited Swansea University for the lectureship that was offered to me after I had completed my Ph.D. .

In fact, during that period I visited my alma mater and simultaneously was undergoing training on Phase Separation Limited's Total Organic Carbon Analyser (TOC). During my tenure with Phase Separation Limited in the UK, I received a letter dated May 19, 1982, from Mr. Thyagarajan of SPINCO Instruments Consortium in Madras, who was CIC's distributor for Southern India. This letter reached me overseas and played an important role in the ongoing dynamics of the business.

Mr. Shrish Patel and his team actively engaged in correspondence and meetings with all the distributors and agents associated with CIC. They employed various tactics and in some instances, their efforts proved successful by offering substantial discounts, nearly 30-40 % of the rates quoted by CIC. In response, I chose not to react to these actions and instead focused on managing my own affairs. I refrained from providing any explanations to my agents and distributors, leaving the decision-making to their discretion.

Despite Mr. Patel's attempts to outcompete, he struggled in the fierce market competition. Eventually, he decided to hand over his company, Sigma Instruments, to his staff to ensure its survival and to continue giving tough competition to CIC. Initially, he transferred ownership to the existing staff and eventually he sold the company to the former production manager of CIC, who continues to operate Sigma Instrument in a low-profile manner. Mr. Patel liquidated his assets, including his house and factory and departed for the UK with all his belongings. Meanwhile, CIC experienced remarkable growth following Mr. Patel's departure. The detailed accounts of CIC and CICPL assets have been discussed in earlier chapters, i.e., Section 10, "The Art of Asset Building."

There is a well-known saying in Hindi that goes: "जो किसी के लिए गड्ढा खोदता है, भगवन उसके लिए खाई खोदता है |" In English, it translates to, "Those who digs a pit for others, falls into it themselves: whoever sets a trap will themselves be caught in it." It serves as a cautionary reminder about the potential repercussions of one's intentions and actions.

The above is fully applicable to Mr. Shrish Patel and Mrs. Saryu Ben Patel.

Part II: An Attack on those Near and Dear

The Kidnap Threats Begin: A Parent's Worst Nightmare

My Kids, Gaurav and Amar

During this period, we received three threatening letters regarding the kidnapping of my children, Gaurav and Amar. The first letter demanded Rs. 2 Lakhs, specifying when and where to deliver the cash – between GIDC and Manjalpur village, under a large tree, at midnight. The letter warned that if the money was not paid, one child would be kidnapped within two days. Fearing for my children's safety, I immediately contacted Colonel Samsher Singh, showed him the letter and sought his advice. Colonel Singh spoke to Police Inspector Chudasama and read the letter on the phone. He also advised me to contact police commissioner Mr. Manmohan Mehta, whom we knew personally. Mr. Mehta assured us of the necessary measures to ensure our children's safety and directed Mr. Chudasama and the Makarpura police station to deploy personnel to apprehend the blackmailers. Mr. Chudasama instructed me to prepare a parcel containing cow dung and place it at the specified location and time according to the letter. Accompanied by Mr. Arun Kochar, a family friend, I went to the site at 4 a.m. to check if the parcel was still there. To our surprise, it was missing. We immediately went to Mr. Chudasama's residence, informed him of the situation and learned that the parcel had been brought to the police station by the Makarpura station team, acting on the instructions of the Police Commissioner.

The next day, we received another similar letter, giving us one more chance to comply with their demands, threatening to kidnap both children if we failed to satisfy them. We promptly handed over this letter to the police and refrained from reacting or leaving anything at the specified location. Members of both police stations suggested that the letters did not appear to be written by professionals and hinted that it could've been the work of one of our ex-employees. However, we chose not to accuse any ex-employee to avoid potential future enmity.

Following the receipt of these threatening letters, my friends speculated that Mr. Shrish Patel, who had lost the company in the auction despite manipulating and misleading the employees, might have assumed I would be unable to pay him the Rs. 5 Lakhs by cheque. Furthermore, when this plan failed, he may have attempted to frighten me into leaving the area for the safety of my children. Subsequently, I began carrying a loaded revolver, hanging it around my neck. I escorted my children to and from school. The school's Principal, Dr. Prasad and Vice Principal, Mr. Bakshi, summoned me to their office, expressing concern about the revolver. After explaining the situation, they advised me to keep the children at home temporarily, as the school could not take responsibility for any potential mishaps. The response from principal and Vice Principal to the revolver and keeping the children at home infuriated me. I expressed my unwillingness to raise my children as cowards, especially considering that I had paid the fees for the entire year. In the face of my anger and resolute stance, they suggested a compromise.

They proposed that I bring the children to school 20 minutes before the usual time, dropping them off in Principal's room. Similarly, I should pick them up 20 minutes before the scheduled departure and collect them from Vice Principal's office. They also requested that I keep the gun out of the children's sight. Despite my initial displeasure, I agreed with their suggestions.

I relayed this dialogue with the school principals to the Police Commissioner (PC) and Colonel Samsher Singh. The PC arranged for a police officer to sit in an auto-rickshaw stationed near the entrance gate of Bhavans, keeping a watch during school hours in the morning and evening. I was informed later that this arrangement continued for about a month without any untoward incidents. Both of my children successfully completed their 12th class studies at this school. Remarkably, in the year 2024, even my two grandchildren also completed their 12th class studies from the same school. As I mentioned above, I am a strong believer in Swami Vivekananda Ji's philosophy and I follow one of his quotes ardently: **"Take up one idea, Make that idea your life. Think of it, dream it, live that idea. This is the way of success."**

By following this advice, I almost saved one year from my allocated time for the Ph.D. After starting my company, I worked about 14-15 hours per day and extensively travelled for marketing and installation. There was no time scheduled for having meals and for rest. I used to travel at night and work in the daytime and because of overworking, I suffered a series of health problems.

The Curse of Overworking: Health Issues Wreak Havoc

In the year 1977, my wife Kiran, sons Gaurav and Amar and I were staying at a hotel in Pahalgam, Kashmir. During our stay, I experienced a sudden fainting spell and collapsed in the bathroom around midnight. The hotel management promptly called Dr. Mirja Ashif Beg, the Medical Officer of the Civil Hospital and Chairman of the N.A.C. Pahalgam. Upon examination, Dr. Beg advised us to immediately return to Jammu and consult a Cardiologist there. This incident is documented in Dr. Beg's inspection note dated October 22nd, 1977.

Following Dr. Beg's recommendation, we returned to Jammu the next morning and proceeded to Varanasi by train. Upon our arrival, I was admitted to the Medical College of BHU. After undergoing medical observation and treatment for 48 hours, I was discharged from the hospital. However, the doctors issued strict instructions that this incident served as a **nature's warning sign**, urging me to prioritise my health and to slow down my pace of life without any delay.

This was a minor heart attack.

It served as a wake-up call, reminding me of the importance of prioritising self-care and well-being. In 2008, I made a visit to the National Institute of Technology (NIT) in Hamirpur, Himachal Pradesh, with the purpose of addressing some educational challenges faced by my nephew, Mr. Davesh Shingari. He was in the third-year of his B.E. in Electronics & Communications at that time. Knowing Professor Raj Kumar Jairal, he arranged accommodations at the NIT guest house on the Hill Top. Arriving at the guest house by taxi from Jalandhar at 6 P.M., I began my discussions with the department the next morning, meeting with the Head of Department and the registrar to resolve Davesh's internship and training concerns. On the second morning of my visit, I decided to go for a morning walk at 5 am. After completing a 4 km downhill walk, I encountered difficulties in breathing while climbing back up the hill towards the guest house.

Sensing something amiss with my heart, I took brief rest breaks but continued to experience breathing issues. Upon returning to the guest house and having breakfast with my friend Prof. Jairal, I recounted the morning's events to him. Together, we made the decision to return to Jalandhar and then Baroda for further medical evaluation. By afternoon, I boarded a train from Jalandhar to Baroda, arriving the next afternoon.

Reflecting on the episode, I became increasingly concerned about the possibility of a cardiovascular issue. To confirm my suspicions, I visited my dentist's office, located on the fourth floor of a multi-storied building in Alkapuri. Opting to take the stairs instead of the lift, I encountered similar breathing difficulties upon reaching the fourth floor, reminiscent of my experience in Hamirpur. Concerned, I contacted Dr. Atul Saxena, a family friend dentist's clinic, who promptly arranged for me to see a Cardiologist at the SSG Hospital, where he was H.O.D of Dept. of Surgery.

Accompanied by my family doctor, Dr. Arvind Iyer and another family friend, Dr. Sailesh Talati, I underwent angiography at Banker's

Heart Institute and Hospital on O.P. Road. The angiography revealed that all three main arteries were 90% blocked. Dr. Darshan Banker, who conducted the test, proposed the installation of 3 stents. He gave us the choice of whether to get it done now or later, as there was no emergency. After careful consideration and consultation with Dr. Talati and Dr. Iyer, I decided to proceed with the stenting procedure right away without any delay.

Two medicine coated stents and one SS stent were successfully installed and I was transferred to a deluxe room where my wife and sons, were waiting anxiously. By the end of the day, I found myself in a room at Banker's Hospital, where I felt uncomfortable. I conveyed my discomfort to the hospital staff, expressing my need for a better room. They proceeded to show me several rooms on the same floor, but none seemed to suit my preferences. Frustrated with the options, I reached out to Mr. Mahesh Idnani, the Income Tax Commissioner at Kota, for assistance. Mahesh assured me that he would resolve the issue and instructed me to wait for ten minutes.

After about twenty minutes, Dr. Mrs. Parul Banker, accompanied by a lovely bouquet, arrived at my room. She inquired about the type of room I was looking for and my wife, Kiran, explained our requirements. Dr. Mrs. Parul Banker then showed us a spacious room that resembled a suite adorned with pleasing décor. It was exactly what we were looking for. Grateful for the assistance, I was promptly shifted to the VIP room, where I stayed for five to six nights. The conducive environment, coupled with the expertise of the cardiologists, contributed to my speedy recovery.

It was later revealed that Dr. Mrs. Parul Banker and her husband, Dr. Darshan Banker, were good friends of Mr. Mahesh Idnani, who had previously served as the Income Tax Commissioner in Baroda. Their connection facilitated my access to the VIP accommodations, ensuring that I received the best possible care during my stay at Banker's Hospital.

In 2019, I found myself once again admitted to Banker's Hospital after experiencing a heart attack in the middle of the night. My wife immediately contacted Dr. Mrs. Parul Banker, who had become a trusted family friend and treated me as if I were her own uncle. Dr. Banker swiftly took charge, instructing my wife to bring me to the hospital while organising the necessary arrangements. Upon our arrival, hospital staff were already waiting outside and wasted no time in rushing me to the ICU on a stretcher. An angiography revealed that one of my arteries was fully blocked, with the blockage located just 1 or 2 mm away from the site of a previous stent insertion. Given the difficulty of installing another stent, the doctor opted to halt the procedure and transferred me to the ICU.

Dr. Mrs. Parul Banker sought assistance from another Cardiologist and together with Dr. Darshan Banker, they performed a challenging stenting operation. Despite the complexity of the procedure, they succeeded in addressing the blockage. However, later that same night, I experienced another severe attack. Sensing the urgency, I instructed my son, Amar, to call the doctors immediately as I felt myself slipping away. Several doctors rushed to my ICU cabin and managed to stabilise my condition, as my blood pressure had plummeted dangerously low. Thanks to the presence of competent medical professionals in the ICU at that critical moment, I survived.

Following a week-long stay in the hospital, I returned home. However, about ten days later, I suffered yet another attack at 4 am. Recognising the signs, I instructed my wife to inform

Dr. Mrs. Parul Banker and immediately prepare for my admission to Banker's Hospital. With swift coordination, arrangements were made in the ICU and once again, I managed to survive the ordeal.

Reflecting on these experiences, it is clear that I have always remained vigilant and sensitive to the symptoms of my cardiovascular condition, enabling me to take timely action and seek appropriate medical care. From 1977 to 2019, these symptoms persisted, underscoring the importance of being proactive about one's health and seeking medical attention when needed and it was given to me on war footing by Banker's doctors.

The Power of Persistence: Another Medical Demon Rears its Head

Ten Days after my second heart attack, operation and stent insertion at Banker's Heart Institute, I developed drug reactions – my lips, left jaw and tongue were swollen and completely filled my mouth. Cardiologists described it as a drug reaction due to one of the latest drugs used. They believed it was an allergic reaction and it was controlled by taking antiallergy medication. However, after ten days, the reaction spread to my entire body and my Cardiologist advised me to contact a Skin Specialist. The Skin Specialist treated me for about 2-3 months by giving me strong anti-biotics and steroids of all types, but it could not be controlled. I consulted many skin specialists, but none of them could solve this problem.

My friend Mr. Kirit Bhai Patel arranged a meeting with two allopathic doctors and two homoeopathic doctors at his farm house. After examining me, all four of them agreed that it was an auto-immune disease - Psoriasis and there was no allopathic cure, however, homoeopathy could cure it. It would take a very long time for recovery from the disease.

I was in a very pitiable state and everybody said that this was an incurable disease. I reached a stage where I was unable to stand and walk on my own, even for 2 minutes! I had to crawl to switch on the light when pricking needles sensation started at night. This happened in Solan. On 18th October 2021, I moved to Government Hospital and after seeing the condition of my body, the doctor declared I had severe psoriasis and started a homoeopathic treatment. This treatment continued till December 2021 and after that, the concerned doctor went on maternity leave. I contacted Dr. Poorav Desai, Principal of the Homoeopathic College of Parul University, Baroda. Now, I have been taking homoeopathic medicine for the last three years without a single break and have recovered up to about 90% – 95 % and the treatment is still going on. I am able to lead my normal life and perform all my duties regularly, including morning walks, exercise and official duties.

I cured myself by observing the following:

1. With a very strong **will** – saying every day that I will be cured.
2. With strong **determination** – saying every day that I will be cured.
3. Taking medicines regularly and giving feedback to the doctor every week.
4. Keep good hygiene, cleansing daily with lukewarm water twice a day.
5. Avoid soap and other chemical detergents, etc.

We (Patient & Doctor) won the so-called "lost battle" and defeated an auto-immune disease – psoriasis – mainly due to strong will power, strong determination and full confidence in my doctor.

Part III: Many Failed Ventures but Ultimately a Successful Man

So far, I have discussed my successful ventures, but in real-life, there are many occasions when you fail in your proposed ventures. I have also failed in the following ventures:

- Moscow Exhibition
- Hotel Amar at Kota.
- Solan food processor at Solan.
- Channel Partners of Johns Chromatography, Wales and Phased Separation, England.

Moscow Exhibition: Failure to Circumvent the System

CIC participated in an International Exhibition in Moscow, USSR, in the year 1980 and booked a small stall in the India Pavilion. My neighbour was M/s Torrent Pharmaceuticals, represented by Mr. Mehta, owner of the company. This was our first visit to the USSR in December. I did not book my hotel through the Indian agents as they were quoting very high prices. I went to Moscow with the intention of booking a room in a low-budget hotel. On arrival at the airport, I came to know that all Indians have to stay in one hotel and cannot go to any other hotel. The hotel bus was waiting at the airport and all Indians boarded the same bus. This bus was exclusively for the exhibitors coming from India. After a failed attempt to book my hotel, I put my baggage on the same bus and reached the hotel along with my wife. I tried my best to book one-room for us but was told that no room was available. All the Indian participants were standing in the queue as there was only one counter. I studied the people standing in the line and found many of them were young.

I contacted a few of them and told them that I had no room to stay in as I had not booked the hotel from India. I requested that if one of them surrendered their room, then I could request the management to allot me the same. Most people were single and two people could share one-room, which would be highly economical and their expenses would be reduced. This idea worked and one person surrendered his room and told the receptionist that he would share the room with another person. I was also with them at the reception and said, "Please allot that room to me." The room was allotted and we stayed there.

Around midnight, I received a call to check that I was Dr. M.K. Shingari, along with

Dr. Mrs. Kiran Shingari. I confirmed that we were the Shingaris and immediately after that, the phone was cut. On enquiring, I learned that since there was no booking in our name, their intelligence wanted to confirm the whereabouts of my family. This is how the USSR was working. The KBG (Russian Abbreviation for State Security Committee) knew all the actions of all individuals there. So, my advice is to always book your hotel from your own country before leaving for any communist country.

We stayed in Moscow for one week when the temperature there was -40 °C. Since this was our first time, we were not equipped with shoes as we thought that we would buy our shoes from Moscow, which were suitable for the temperature there. We failed to exchange our traveller's cheque from the Bank of Baroda with the Russian currency - Rubels. Because we had no money, we could not purchase shoes and walked in Indian sandals. The exchanger authority advised us to get our cheque attested by the Indian High Commissioner and after that they would accept our cheques.

We took a bus from the hotel to the High Commissioner's Office which was 10 km away. We had to walk in the snow at -40°C in our sandals and our feet were frozen. My wife was regularly complaining that she could not feel her feet and was unable to walk. I kept on repeatedly saying, "Presume there is a war between India and Pakistan and we have to cross the border to save our lives."

With this, she got a lot of moral support as I was telling her that to save our lives, we have to forget everything else. Finally, we reached the High Commissioner's Office, where we were attended very gracefully. The High Commissioner was surprised that we could walk with very ordinary Indian sandals in these temperatures. He asked us to put up our feet on the settee and instructed his staff to put up two heaters directly facing our feet for each of us. He even offered us some hot coffee. They did their best to bring our feet to normal temperature. They very much appreciated our courage to walk in these temperatures. The High Commissioner certified our cheques and ultimately, we received the cash and could complete our shopping. The Newscaster of All India Radio in Moscow, was one Sardarji gentleman from Punjab, who took good care of us apart from guiding.

Exhibitors from India

Photograph with Indian High Commissioner

Regarding the exhibition, it was announced that the Vice President of the USSR would be visiting the Indian Pavilion and all should be present in their stalls. Dr. (Mrs.) Kiran Shingari and myself were waiting the whole day and did not observe any extraordinary dignitary visit our stall. I asked Mr. Mehta of Torrent Ahmedabad when the Vice President was coming and he told me that he had come and gone. Then I told him that there was no security or anything abnormal to feel that the Vice President was passing our stall. He said that he had come along with 2-3 people in plain clothes to yours as well as my stall. At the end of the exhibition, I said to Mr. Mehta, “Nobody has placed any order or made any inquiry about our product.”

His reply was shocking. “If you want to sell your product in this country, you have to appoint an agent or liaison officer, pay a handsome amount of commission, which includes everything and only after that will you get the inquiries and eventually orders,” he said. “You cannot sell your product without giving a commission.”

After this, we visited Moscow again for another exhibition and again failed to get any order from the USSR.

Hotel Amar: Failure to Tolerate Harassment

This is my second failed venture. I constructed Hotel Amar with fifteen rooms on the first floor of Shri Pukhraj Jain's building at the Aerodrome Circle at Kota. I purchased the facility by using Mr. Jain's roof on an ownership basis after making a reasonable payment. On my roof, Mr. Jain had full rights and I could not do anything about that. I employed Mr. Pannalal, Mr. Jain's son-in-law, as the manager. He used to ring me any time during the night as he was bothered by Mr. Chopra, Superintendent of the Excise Department, insisting on undesirable and unacceptable demands like the supply of liquor or women late at night. Mr. Chopra used his authority and even after I spoke to him, he kept on chanting, *"Pannalal, tu kutta hai, hum Panjabiyon mein ghar jamai ko kutta bolte hai. You should live separately as an independent person and not with in-laws."*

I felt that by upsetting my manager, he used to gain some perverse pleasure. Being a scientist, I could not tolerate frequent disturbed nights and finally had to close down my hotel in Kota.

Solan Food Processors: Failure to Diversify into Consumer Products

This is my 3rd failed project. I opened a partnership company by the name of Solan Food Processors to manufacture "Natural Organic Honey." My partner was Dr. Kailash Prashar, the gentleman from whom I purchased the land and building. The idea was to collect the natural honey from the Himachal Belt and process it as organic honey for export to Europe. I negotiated with a French company during one of my visits to France to supply them with organic honey. They gave me a blanket order for 10 tonnes of honey. I accepted the order without discussing the price and other terms and conditions, but their assurance was that they would buy a whole lot of honey, which ought to be in line with Europe's norms for organic products.

I thought that Himachal jungles must be supplying 100% pure organic honey as this is not an agricultural state using pesticides and insecticides. I requested my cousin's brother, Lt. Anil Kumar Sarin, to collect honey from faraway villages. We collected more than 10 tonnes of honey and shifted the same to Baroda for processing.

In Baroda, one company was manufacturing food products for "Parle," and I contacted their owner, who agreed to process the same and give me the final product in packed condition in 200 mL, 400 mL and 500 mL glass bottles. I sent 12 500 mL bottles of honey to the company in Paris. They got it tested in two labs: one in-house and the other from outside the company.

They approved our product.

I was very happy and satisfied that our organic honey was approved. On my request, they offered a price which was even less than my manufactured product. I opened all my cards to them but they offered their inability to reconsider the price structure. This gave me a big shock as I thought they were taking advantage of my ignorance and simplicity with the impression that ultimately, I would surrender. I refused to supply the honey at their price and closed the deal.

After my intention to export organic honey failed, I decided to sell it in the Indian market. We started marketing in Baroda on a trial basis and gave 12 200 mL bottles of pure organic honey to about ten dealers and shopkeepers on a trial basis. All of them took 400 mL and 500 mL at a fixed price and we supplied it to them. They assured us that we could collect the payment after 15 days. We contacted all of them and to our surprise not a single shopkeeper or dealer gave us the money and said, "Come after five days."

We went again after five days and they were still finding some excuse for not making the payment immediately, as agreed. I had never dealt with a consumer market. Usually, my dealings were with top people like Scientists, the owner of the company and other technical people where dealings and commitments were honoured.

I realised after some time that the consumer market was not my cup of tea and decided to pull out. My stock of 10 tonnes of honey was lying with me for about 20 years and even after that I could not sell and suffered a big loss.

My conclusion was that being a Scientist, I should remain in my scientific field and should not venture into other businesses like consumer goods and low-cost products including laboratory instruments.

Summary

Section 8: The Absolute Cost of Success and Ambition

Major incidents:

1. The betrayal of CIC partner, Mr. Shrish Patel and the subsequent auction of the company.
2. The toll of overworking on personal health and family.
3. The power of learning from failed ventures such as the Moscow Exhibit, Hotel Amar and Solan Food Processors.

Learning:

1. Trust but verify. Always acknowledge the power of your instincts. Be wary of the unknown foes.
2. Prioritise your health along with professional commitments. As the famous Hindi proverb goes, "*Sar salamat toh pagadi pachas.*"
3. Set a good example in front of future generations and never compromise on your principles.

4. Do not let failure define you. Learn from it and advance in your career with courage and compassion.

Chapter defining quote:

"I am a strong believer in Swami Vivekananda Ji and I follow one of his quotes ardently: 'Take up one idea, Make that idea your life. Think of it, dream it and live that idea. This is the way to success.'"

Section 9

Growing in Leaps and Bounds Towards Unprecedented Success

"Stand up, be bold, be strong, take the whole responsibility on yourself and know that you are the creator of your own destiny."

Part I: Inception and Evolution of CIC's R&D Unit

The In-House Research & Development Centre of Chromatography & Instruments Company has been consistently recognised since 1982 (Registration No. Tu/N – Rd/820) by the Department of Scientific & Industrial Research, Ministry of Science & Technology, Government of India, New Delhi. Notably, our R&D centre bears the registration number 820, indicating that until 1982, there were only 820 recognised units and we proudly stand among them.

IN HOUSE RESEARCH & DEVELOPMENT CENTER
CHROMATOGRAPHY & INSTRUMENTS COMPANY
RECOGNIZED SINCE 1982 WITHOUT ANY BREAK (TU/N – RD/820)
By
Department of scientific & Industrial Research
Ministry of Science & Technology
GOI, New Delhi – 110016

OUR RESEARCH & DEVELOPMENT CENTER

The Research and Development wing of CIC was established on the first floor of the company, featuring a separate entrance and staff dedicated to enhancing existing products and modifying our standard products to align with the specific applications of users. The Government actively encouraged Industrialists to establish their R&D units, promoting the improvement of existing products and the development of new ones to foster innovation in the industrial sector.

The Central Government offered the following concessions with conditions:

1. The registration will be valid for the period specified in the registration letter. The renewal of registration should be sought whenever the renewal of recognition for the In-house R&D unit is granted.

2. The registration will authorise the In-house R&D unit to avail customs/ Central Excise duty exemptions on the import/ purchase of equipment, instruments, spares, consumables, etc., during the recognised period, subject to the relevant Government policies in force. Exemptions need to be separately applied in the prescribed formats. The In-house R&D units must comply with the terms and conditions of customs and Central excise notifications issued or amended from time to time.

3. The registration of the In-house R&D unit by DSIR does not automatically grant customs/ central excise duty exemptions. Institutions seeking such exemptions must apply separately to the customs/ central excise authorities.

4. In the event of disposal or sale of R&D equipment, clearance from customs/ excise authorities will be required, considering the applicable notifications under which the equipment was imported or purchased in India.

The recognition of our R&D centre brought several benefits, particularly in fostering collaboration with Government Organisations such as the Department of Atomic Energy, the Ministry of Defence and numerous CSIR Laboratories. This recognition facilitated the exchange of technological ideas and the sharing of technical details. Additionally, it provided access to technical papers and encouraged data sharing with other organisations that may not typically interact.

The uninterrupted renewal of our R&D wing at CIC for 40 years attests to the appreciation of our set-up and the import substitute instrumentation developed by our centre. Following the nuclear device explosion at Pokhran, restrictions were imposed by the USA, Japan and Europe on the import of hi-tech instruments needed for research in Atomic Energy establishments and CSIR research labs. Despite these challenges, our company supplied similar instruments at significantly lower prices, contributing to locally available and substantial savings for organisations like BARC, IGCAR and Ordnance factories, which were under embargo.

Our R&D efforts have played a remarkable role in the **Make in India initiative**, resulting in significant savings in foreign exchange over our existence.

As the Director of CIC R&D, I worked alongside my wife, serving as the group leader. Both Kiran and I hold Ph.D.'s from prestigious universities – she from BHU and myself from the University of Wales, UK. Unfortunately, our R&D recognition has not been renewed since 2021 due to challenges in complying with the revised rules of the Government of India. The new instructions specify recognition only for private limited and limited companies, while CIC operates as a proprietary company owned by me. We have conveyed to the Director of DST that CIC, with over 50 years of history and a recognised R&D centre for the past 40 years, has accumulated assets that cannot be easily transferred to a private limited company due to Income Tax considerations. Our commitment is to adhere to the law and we faced challenges in converting to a private limited company within the stipulated timeframe.

Despite our efforts, our application for the renewal of recognition of In-house R&D beyond March 31, 2021, was influenced by the Government of India's policy and not due to any other reasons. The Director of the DST, Dr. Desh Pandey, tried his best to help us with two six-month extensions each, but he was helpless in convincing the authorities to exempt our company. I take pride in highlighting that **CIC stands as a unique entity in India, being one of only three companies globally** specialising in the production of advanced import substitute analysers tailored for Atomic Energy Establishments and nuclear plants.

Some of these are as follows:

1. Hydrogen Determinator (priced at around Rs. 45,00,000/- each)
2. Oxygen Nitrogen Determinator (priced at around Rs. 50,00,000/-)
3. HON Determinator (priced at around Rs. 85,00,000/- each)
4. On-Line Process GC (priced at around Rs. 35,00,000/- onwards)

5. Carbon Sulphur Determinator (priced at around Rs. 30,00,000/-)

Due to our proficiency in manufacturing the aforementioned analysers, we have consistently extended our support to various Ordnance Factories by analysing their urgent samples during the production of arsenals. Enclosed herewith are copies of letters of appreciation received from Indian ordnance factories acknowledging our valuable contributions. Two of which are mentioned below:

Jt. General Manager, Ordnance Factory, Ambajhari, Nagpur – 440021.

Jt. General Manager, Field Gun Factory, Kalpi Road, Kanpur – 208009.

Our company continues to maintain its R&D centre, functioning with the same commitment and dedication as before. We take pride in our ongoing contributions to Indian Ordnance Factories and Research Organisations. Our unwavering commitment to innovation and technological advancements reflects our dedication to providing valuable support to critical sectors. We are immensely proud of our contributions to various industries and our commitment remains steadfast.

For detailed information on the products developed by our research centre, please refer to our website – www.chromatographyinst.com. Our website offers comprehensive details about the innovative products and solutions developed through our ongoing Research and Development efforts. It is worth noting that despite potential challenges, I chose to uphold the principles and maintain transparency in the renewal process of our In-house recognition. Rather than resorting to manipulating accounts or providing misleading information to the Department of Scientific and Industrial Research (DST) authorities, I remained steadfast and honest, choosing not to compromise on ethical standards. However, my company has developed the following products, most of which are **import substitutes**. This is another proof that CIC started following the slogan of our Prime Minister Shri Modi ji – **MAKE IN INDIA.**

Research & Development Innovation

Are Root Cause Of Our Success & Survival

For 49 Years

Sr. No.	Instrument	Year
1.	Hydrogen Determinator with Infrared Detector	2012
2.	Diffusible Hydrogen Analyser	2012
3.	GC configured as TOGA as per ASTM D 3612-C; Fully Automated Version	2013
4.	GC configured as TOGA as per ASTM D 3612-C; Manual Version	2013
5.	GC & Online GC based on Ionisation Detector	2013
6.	Oxygen – Hydrogen Determinator	2014
7.	HON Determinator	2015
8.	Basic Model of C-S Determinator	2015
9.	C-S Determinator fully automatic software-controlled system	2016
10.	Commercialisation of Analogue Integrator	2017
11.	C-S Determinator fully automatic software-controlled system for radioactive samples of BARC, IGCAR &ordnance factories	2017
12.	New FID Design for improved SN ratio and lower manufacturing cost	2018
13.	Launch of New Version of DGA interpretation software suitable for 64-bit Windows environment	2018
14.	Automatic DGA Analyser without using Mercury for extraction of gases for transformer oil.	2020

Part II: Establishing Roots in Solan and Bridging the North-South Divide

Conquering the Foothills of the Himachal: Setting Up an Industry in Solan

In the year 1993, the Himachal Pradesh Government offered lucrative incentives to encourage industrialists and individuals to establish manufacturing units in the state. The various concessions provided by both the State and Central Governments were particularly appealing to me.

Some of the key incentives and attractions included:

1. No Income Tax for five years after at concessional rates for another five years.
2. No sales tax for five years.
3. No excise duty for five years.

In addition to the aforementioned incentives, there were several more attractive offerings, such as subsidised electric power supply, investment subsidies and industrial plots at concessional rates in the designated industrial areas. Encouraged by these favourable conditions, I decided to establish a partnership company in

Solan, Himachal Pradesh (HP). My familiarity with the Solan District stemmed from my initial employment in Kasauli at the Central Serum Research Institute.

During my suspension from the institute, some of my classmates from Delhi University and I sought refuge in Solan. I had acquaintances there, including Dr. Kailash Prashar and Dr. Mrs. Lalita Prashar. Dr. Mrs.Lalita Prashar was a former MBBS student at Meerut Medical College and Dr. Rukma Idnani served as the principal there. They were particularly instrumental in connecting me with the right people. Dr. Rukma Idnani, introduced me to her favourite student, Dr. Mrs. Lalita Prashar who, along with her husband, Dr. Kailash Prashar, had a hospital and residence in the heart of Solan.

The Prashar family was one of the richest families in the area. Dr. Kailash Prashar was also the General Secretary of the Indian National Congress of Himachal Pradesh. Having decided to establish a small industrial unit in Solan to take advantage of the Government benefits, I discussed my plans with the Prashars, who generously offered their help and support. They even welcomed me to stay with them until suitable accommodation was found.

In 1993, we secured a two-room rental accommodation in the village of Rabon, at the residence of Mrs. Kamla Devi. To spearhead the groundwork, we stationed Mr.Bharat Bhushan, an employee from Baroda, he moved to Solan with his wife. They played a crucial role in initiating the necessary paperwork and successfully registered our partnership company under the name "Precision Scientific Instruments" with the General Manager of the District Industry Centre in Chambaghat, Solan.

Aided by our CIC accounts officer, Mr. Vipin Vohra, we submitted a comprehensive project report outlining our plans for the manufacturing of laboratory scientific instruments and software-based data processors, with a focus on developing small hardware for interfacing data processors with GCs and other analytical instruments. We filed the Income Tax return for the financial year 1993-94 and our case underwent scrutiny, lasting for three years until 1997.

During this period, we acquired a plot of approximately 900 square metres on the Kalka–Shimla highway, initially part of NH22 and now on NH5. Given that the plot fell under Anji village Panchayat, which is classified as a rural area, we were not eligible to buy land without proper permission. To address this, we purchased the land in the name of Dr. Kailash Prashar. The plan approval for the factory/ house was sought under Dr. Prashar's name and it was granted by the Panchayat. In Himachal Pradesh, outsiders are prohibited from acquiring agricultural land in rural areas without the State Government's permission, as per Section 118. We applied for this permission from the Ministry of Revenue, Government of Himachal Pradesh, Shimla.

The construction of the house-cum-factory was entrusted to Sardar Pyara Singh, an honest contractor from Solan, in 1993. The building, spanning five stories, began with the completion of two basement floors in 1994, prompting our move from Rabon to our new facility. The remaining three floors were completed in 1995. While we had not received Governmental permission for land purchase and construction, our building was finished and we obtained electrical and water connections from the relevant authorities in the name of Dr. Kailash Prashar.

Subsequently, we received a notice from the District Collector (DC) of Solan regarding **illegal construction**, with the threat of **confiscation** under Section 118 for building without the permission of the Government. In our response to the DC's letter, we asserted that the land and building belonged to Dr. Kailash Parashar and we had acquired it on a rental basis. The DC demanded proof of Dr. Prashar's ownership, pointing out that the funds used for land purchase and construction were from the company's current bank account.

The case went to court and after approximately one year, the decision came in our favour, accepting Dr. Prashar's ownership of the land and building. However, the DC imposed a condition prohibiting Dr. Prashar from selling the building to me or my family members. We justified in court that we were waiting for the Government's permission to purchase the land and in the absence of approval, had requested a family friend from Himachal Pradesh to buy the plot and construct the building as per our specifications. An agreement was signed and registered, stating that Precision Scientific Instruments (PSI) would lease the constructed building and land from Dr. Prashar. PSI would make all payments on behalf of Dr. Prashar as an advance, reflecting the land and building in his Income Tax return, with the amount paid by PSI considered as an advance/ loan for construction, to be adjusted against the rent. We contested the DC's order and appealed to the Revenue Commissioner in Shimla. The final decision favoured us, stating that the **District Collector had no jurisdiction to decide whom to sell or not sell to;** it was beyond his authority. After the issuance of the aforementioned order, the threat of confiscation was withdrawn and Dr. Prashar regained full ownership of the land and building. He thereby gained the authority to sell it to any party of his choice. This incident occurred during the tenure of the Congress party in Himachal Pradesh. Then, the Bharatiya Janta Party (BJP) came to power and **Shri Narendrabhai Modi** was overseeing the state of Himachal Pradesh. During Mr. Modi's visit, Dr. Bindal, the BJP head of Solan District, informed us that Mr. Modi was in Mohali, Chandigarh and suggested that we reach out to him for assistance.

Barodian roots meet in the Mountains: Meeting Shri Narendra Modi

Upon contacting Mr. Modi, the then BJP Prabhari for the State of Himachal Pradesh, I introduced myself and requested an appointment to discuss the challenges we were facing with our small establishment in Solan. Mr. Modi inquired about the subject of discussion and I explained that we were from Baroda, Gujarat, with a few decades-old factories in GIDC, Baroda and had recently started a small factory in Solan, encountering various issues that required his support. Mr. Modi inquired about who had accompanied me from Gujarat and I replied that my younger son Amar had come with me. Then, Mr. Modi suggested, "You better send Amar here at 11 A.M. in Mohali."

Amar went to Mohali as scheduled and upon arrival, found Mr. Modi sitting on a mattress on the floor. He shared the events that led up to the confiscation of our factory-cum-residence building by the previous government. Mr. Modi attentively listened to the concerns and read the detailed representation made with the CM's intervention and help.

After reviewing the representation, Mr. Modi wrote a note on top of the front page, instructing Dr. Bindal, District President of BJP in Solan to assist Gujarat's industrialist Dr. Shingari to set-up an industry in Himachal Pradesh. Amar informed Mr. Modi about the challenges we faced and Mr. Modi remarked, "You could have gone to Kutch or Gandhinagar, where all benefits of a backward area are given to the electronics industry."

Despite the challenges, Amar emphasised that we chose Himachal Pradesh to benefit from the backward area incentives. Mr. Modi suggested meeting Dr. Bindal, who would assist us further.

We met Dr. Bindal and he assured us that the best course of action was to reapply. Following Dr. Bindal's guidance, we reapplied for the purchase of the land and the building, eventually obtaining permission from the Himachal Pradesh Government. We continued running Precision Scientific Instruments for six years, availing ourselves of all the benefits of the backward area. After six years, the company went into a low-profile with reduced sales.

On May 23, 1999, the partners of PSI, along with another individual, jointly formed a new company named Himachal Instrumentation Private Limited. This company operated for four years until September 30, 2003, utilising benefits offered by the State and Central Governments. We applied to the Registrar of Companies at Jallandar to close down this Private Limited Company and the request was granted. Income Tax returns were filed up to March 31, 2004.

Driven by a persistent pursuit of opportunities, we registered a new company for the third time, Chromatography and Analyzers Company, effective from October 11, 2004. This company operated until September 30, 2013, benefiting from Income Tax, Sales Tax, Excise Duty and Service Tax Incentives.

Following the expiration of these benefits, we closed down Chromatography and Analyzers Company on September 30, 2013. Our very first company, Precision Scientific Instruments, continues to operate, holding all the properties in Solan under its name. It's essential to highlight the challenges we faced during the early years of our venture in Solan, particularly with the Income Tax Department, Sales Tax Department and Excise Department.

These authorities were sceptical of recognising PSI as a manufacturing company, forming the opinion that we were merely involved in billing and manipulating accounts to evade income tax. The IT authorities conducted a raid on our company's premises, seizing all the books of our accounts, purchases and sales registers. They asserted that we were not entitled to the benefits provided to backward areas and insisted on us paying the Income Tax, Sales Tax and Excise Duty similar to any other unit outside the backward area.

They adamantly denied acknowledging our status as a manufacturer. In response to this situation, we approached the Chief Commissioner of Income Tax, whose office was located in Patiala. Our contact with him was facilitated through the President of the Chamber of Commerce and Industry, Bombay, who was a close friend of Mr. Ahluwalia, the Chief Commissioner of Income Tax for Himachal Pradesh.

Kiran and I met Mr. Ahluwalia at his residence, presenting our case in detail. At the end of the meeting, he instructed us to visit his office at 11 A.M. We followed his advice and he called the Income Tax Officer (ITO) at the Solan Office, instructing him to look into the matter again. He assured us that if any issues persist, we should not hesitate to approach him. Mr. Ahluwalia also shared that he had previously served as the Income Tax Commissioner at Jamnagar and expressed his admiration for the Gujarati people.

Subsequently, we met the ITO at his office, conveying Mr. Ahluwalia's guidance. The ITO at Solan told us that he had understood the case and was forwarding it to the Deputy Commissioner of Income Tax at Shimla. He also advised us that we should visit the Commissioner of Income Tax (CIT) of Shimla and explain our case in detail, citing that the matter was no longer in his hands and the file had been forwarded to the Deputy Commissioner of Income Tax, Mr. Chopra, in Shimla.

Following this intervention, our case was cleared and an IT order was issued recognising our unit as a manufacturing entity, exempting us from income tax and making us eligible for other incentives as per Government rules.

This was a significant relief for us.

The decision to move to Himachal Pradesh proved to be immensely beneficial, as a majority of our capital was accumulated there, with no taxes applicable. The profits we made remained with us, significantly increasing our working capital. After three decades of operating companies like PSI, we now possess substantial assets, including two five-story buildings comprising a total of twelve apartments with branded lifts.

Bridging Faith and Practicality: Constructing the Solan Mandir Paanch Parmeshwar

In the area where our building stands, accidents were frequent due to the steep, blind curve of the road and lack of proper lighting, leading to its reputation as a **haunted area**. To address this, I decided to build a temple at that corner where accidents often occur. Constructing the temple required building downward four stories to reach road level, resulting in a five-story structure. The templc was designed with columns of varying heights to accommodate idols and allow worshippers to keep their shoes on as the area experiences cold weather. Since the temple's construction, accidents in the area have significantly reduced.

I believe that the temple, situated on the fifth floor with illuminated idols and lights facing the highway and railway track, has contributed to much safer driving conditions in the area. Drivers slow down and pay their respects to the temple as they approach the blind turn. Additionally, we've converted a floor above road level into a temple with idols of various deities, with further plans to convert three more floors into temples - a Jain temple, a Multi-religion temple and the last floor for the priest and caretaker.

This temple, named **Solan Mandir Paanch Parmeshwar**, in memory of my father, Shri Sohan Lal Ji Shingari, houses idols of Vaishno Devi Mata, Ganpati Bappa, Shivji and Parvati, Bajrangbali and Saraswati Mata. This temple has become a landmark of Solan.

The Paanch Parmeshwar Temple: A Landmark of Solan

Connecting the North and the South: Sales and Services Offices in the Two Cardinal Directions of India

We commenced our expansion into the northern region by establishing our office for sales and servicing of our instruments. To facilitate this endeavour, we acquired a plot of land in Noida, situated in the Gautam Budh Nagar district of Uttar Pradesh, from the Noida authorities. With the necessary approvals in hand, we embarked on the construction of a combined house and office building in Sector 30 of Noida.

The process involved careful planning and adherence to regulatory requirements, ensuring that our construction project complied with all local regulations and standards. Once the construction plan was approved, we proceeded with the development, mindful of creating a functional and aesthetically pleasing space to serve as both our office and residence. Our newly constructed office-cum-residence in Sector 30 of Noida is a testament to our commitment to expanding our presence in the northern region of India. We take pride in showcasing the architectural and functional aspects of our office through pictorial representations, capturing the essence of our establishment in this vibrant and growing area.

Noida Office-cum-Residence

We hired two Engineers, one with a degree and the other with a diploma, to handle the servicing and marketing of our CIC products in the new office we established. Despite receiving full support from our Headquarters in Baroda, this office struggled to secure orders. Unfortunately, due to the lack of success in procuring orders, we made the difficult decision to close down the office and relocate our staff.

Similarly, we attempted to establish an office in Coimbatore with our former Production

Manager, Mr. Radha Krishnan, at the helm. Operating from a rented house in Coimbatore, Mr. Radha Krishnan successfully managed the office for approximately three years. We were doing very well in South India. Mr. Radha Krishnan got many orders for our products from the area. Unfortunately and tragically, his sudden demise led to the closure of the office.

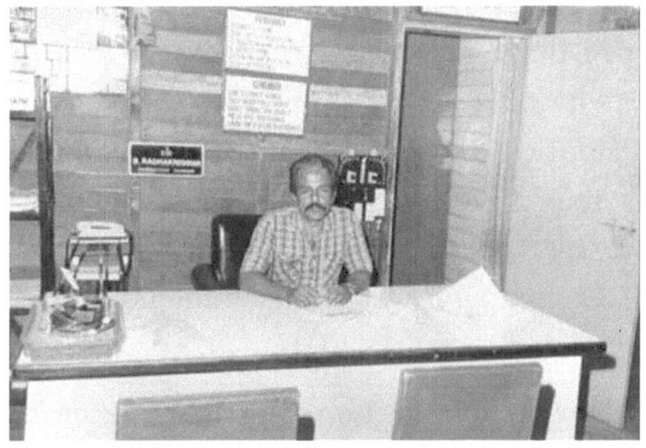

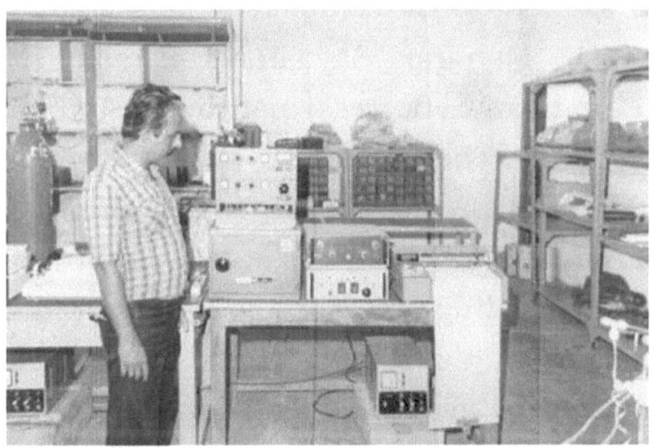

Mr. Radhakrishnan in the Coimbatore Office

Part III: Transitioning from Sole Proprietorship to Partnership

On my 76th birthday, I made the decision to transition my proprietary company into a partnership by involving my two sons, Gaurav Shingari and Amar Shingari, who had been dedicatedly working for the company for the past 25 years. In order for them to become part of the company, I gifted Gaurav and Amar Rs. 47,60,484/- towards their capital contribution and allocated 20% of the shares of the company to each of them. This step officially welcomed both Gaurav and Amar as partners of the Chromatography and Instruments Company, effective from April 1, 2016.

Allow me to reflect on the past three decades. Gaurav and Amar completed their graduation from The Maharaja Sayajirao University (MSU) at Baroda with degrees in B.Com. And B.Sc., respectively. They were then admitted to pursue further studies, with Gaurav enrolling in M.Com. and Amar in M.Sc. Physics at MSU itself. During a family meeting, we collectively discussed their academic pursuits and future career paths. Considering my advancing age and health concerns, particularly my cardiovascular issues dating back to 1977, which led to heart surgery in 2007, where three stents were implanted in my arteries, I was advised to minimise travel and reduce working hours.

Considering the challenges of our business and my health concerns, I presented both Gaurav and Amar with a choice: either discontinue their post-graduation studies and join the company immediately or pursue further education with the understanding that I would not be able to provide them with training in this highly technical field. Emphasising the demanding nature of the Industry, I shared the example of my younger brother, Shri Surinder Kumar Shingari, who was sent to England to work for Jones Chromatography Limited. Despite three years there, he struggled to grasp the intricacies of Chromatography independently. Upon his return to India, he joined CIC but was unable to meet the standards I expected, leading to his termination. This incident illustrated to Gaurav and Amar the rigorous standards I upheld in business.

Upon hearing this, both Gaurav and Amar decided to leave their post-graduation studies and join the company. They started as employees and later became junior partners, though the majority of the shares remained with me. Extensive training was provided, covering technical and non-technical aspects and they worked diligently to learn all the facets of the business, including manufacturing, marketing, accounting and personnel management. Their dedication and hard work have increased the company's turnover manifolds.

Currently, my involvement in CIC's operations is minimal. I've made it clear to Gaurav and Amar that I won't intervene as long as the company remains profitable, but I cannot tolerate any downturn.

Throughout my 52 years of business experience, I've learned that **hard work and discipline are essential for success. While hard work can compensate for a lack of intelligence to some extent, discipline is non-negotiable.** Your actions are closely observed by those around you, including colleagues and employees.

In conclusion, the progress and reputation of our company reflect the effective training provided to them and of hard work of Gaurav and Amar. I am confident that with their continued dedication and disciplined approach, the company will continue to thrive and grow.

These two quotes by Swami Vivekanand Ji are very close to my heart:

"Take up one idea, make that one idea your life. Think of it, dream of it, live on that idea... that is the way to success."

"Stand up, be bold, be strong, take the whole responsibility on yourself and know that you are the creator of your own destiny."

My personal advice, primarily based on my education, experience and vast travel exposure in sixteen countries, a majority of Indian states and along with my large-scale interactions with people from all sections of society, is that officers and owners of the organisation must undergo training in "Leadership and Organisational Behaviour." This course should cover the following topics:

1. Leadership
2. Teamwork
3. Human behaviour
4. Motivation
5. Stress management
6. Perception
7. Communication

The key persons of Chromatography & Instruments Company and Chromatography & Instruments Company Pvt. Ltd. are Dr. M.K. Shingari, Mr. Gaurav Shingari and Mr. Amar Shingari.

DR. M.K. Shingari,
Chairman & Managing Director of CIC Pvt.
Sr. Partner of CIC

Mr. Gaurav Shingari,
Sales Director of CIC Pvt.
Partner of CIC

Mr. Amar Shingari,
Technical Director of CIC Pvt.
Partner of CIC

Part IV: Activating CIC Pvt. Ltd. for Distributorship & Trading

Chromatography and Instruments Company Pvt. Ltd. was officially registered and established in December 1975, with Dr. M.K. Shingari and Mr. Shrish Patel serving as the original Directors. Over the time, the composition of the Board of Directors evolved and presently includes Dr. M.K. Shingari, Dr. Kiran Shingari, Mr. Vipin Vohra, Mr. Gaurav Shingari and Mr. Amar Shingari. However, for several years following its inception, the company remained dormant, with no active operations or revenue generation. From 1975 until 2008, the company consistently reported zero income.

In 2008, a significant development occurred when we were appointed as a channel partner of GE Digital Energy, a reputable multinational corporation headquartered in the USA and UK, with an Indian presence in Bangalore and Baroda. Our role as a channel partner involved facilitating orders from GE Bangalore and GE UK, particularly for substantial orders and purchasing products from them for distribution to our customers across India. Additionally, we would undertake responsibilities such as installation, commissioning and servicing of the equipment supplied by us.

To ensure proficiency in handling GE's range of products, one of our Directors and an Engineer underwent comprehensive training at GE's UK plant, focusing on installation and maintenance procedures. This training equipped us with the necessary skills and knowledge to effectively service and support the GE products we distribute.

Over the years, we have actively participated in GE's Channel Partners Meet, held annually in various locations such as the UK, Bangalore, Goa, Gurgaon and many others. Our consistent efforts and contributions have been recognised through multiple awards bestowed upon us during these events. A selection of these awards is showcased below, reflecting our commitment to excellence and outstanding performance as a channel partner of GE Digital Energy.

2017 Channel Partner's Meet

Our company was recognised as the best promoter of Monitoring and Diagnostics (M&D) products. This accolade reflects our dedication and effectiveness in promoting and advocating for M&D products within our market segment.

2018 Channel Partner's Meet

Our company received a prestigious honour in recognition of our outstanding work on ageing fleet/spec-in for Monitoring and Diagnostics (M&D). This recognition underscores our commitment to excellence and innovation in addressing challenges related to ageing fleet management and specification integration.

2019 Channel Partner's Meet

Our company was presented with an Appreciation Certificate, acknowledging our contributions and efforts in advancing the goals and objectives of the partnership. This certificate serves as a testament to our ongoing commitment to collaboration and mutual success.

2022 Channel Partner's Meet

CIC Pvt. Ltd. was awarded as an outstanding partner. This recognition highlights our exceptional performance, dedication and contributions to the success of the partnership and the overall objectives of the meet. We were honoured to receive this prestigious award, which motivated us to continue striving for excellence in all aspects of our partnership with GE Digital Energy.

Our turnover from 2008 till 2024 has increased considerably and to the satisfaction of our Channel Partner GE.

As a heavy Taxpayer, we have consistently fulfilled our Tax obligations, resulting in numerous letters of appreciation from various Government Departments. This impressive growth trajectory commenced following the retirement of our partner and Director, Mr. Shrish Patel, in 1978. Since our inception in 1972, we have taken great pride in maintaining an impeccable record of compliance with State and Central Government Departments, including Income Tax, Sales Tax, Excise Department and Service Tax, among others.

Throughout the years, both CIC and CIC Pvt. Ltd., along with our Partners and Directors, have received numerous letters of appreciation from the Ministry of Finance for our consistent and timely payment of Income Tax and GST. These commendations serve as a testament to our commitment to fiscal responsibility and adherence to regulatory requirements. A sample copy of our latest certificate of appreciation is enclosed for reference.

From The Central Board of Direct Taxes – 2016-17, 2019-20 for Kiran Shingari, 2016-17, 2019-20 for Gaurav Shingari, 2016-17, 2018-19 for Amar Shingari and 2019-20, 2017-18, 2018-19 for Poonam Shingari.

From The Ministry of Finance up to the year ending March 2021, year ending 2021-22 for payment of GST regularly, for Chromatography & Instruments Company Pvt. Ltd.

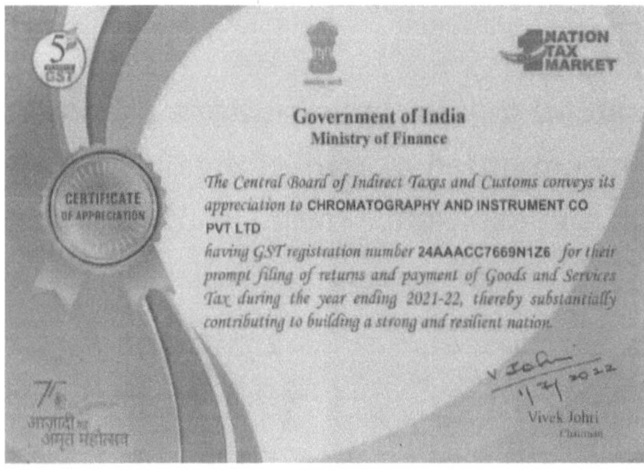

NATION TAX MARKET

CERTIFICATE OF APPRECIATION

Government of India
Ministry of Finance

The Central Board of Indirect Taxes and Customs conveys its appreciation to CHROMATOGRAPHY AND INSTRUMENT CO PVT LTD *having GST registration number* 24AAACC7669N1Z6 *for their prompt filing of returns and payment of Goods and Services Tax during the year ending 2021-22, thereby substantially contributing to building a strong and resilient nation.*

Vivek Johri
Chairman

CERTIFICATE OF APPRECIATION

Ministry of Finance
Government of India
Central Board of Direct Taxes

This is to certify that Mr/Ms KIRAN MAHENDRAKUMAR SHINGARI *(PAN:* AFOPS8337P*) has paid taxes for the Assessment Year* 2019-20 *and filed the Income Tax return. We appreciate the taxpayer, in the 'Silver' category, in recognition of the contribution towards building this great Nation.*

P C Mody
Chairman

In conclusion, it is worth mentioning that the remarkable growth detailed above occurred after the retirement of Mr. Shrish Patel and my family assuming greater autonomy and control. With Mr. Patel's departure, there was a newfound freedom to steer the company's direction and operations in alignment with our vision and values. This transition marked a pivotal moment in our journey, allowing us to implement strategies and initiatives that propelled the company towards unprecedented growth and success. We are grateful for the opportunities presented and remain committed to continuing this trajectory of growth and excellence in the years to come.

Summary

Section 9: Growing in Leaps and Bounds Towards Unprecedented Success

Major incidents:

1. Inception and evolution of CIC's R&D unit in Baroda. The toll of overworking on personal health and family.
2. Establishing roots in Solan, Himachal Pradesh and bridging the North-South divide.
3. Transitioning from sole proprietorship to partnership of CIC Pvt. Ltd.
4. Activating CIC Pvt. Ltd. for distributorship and trading to further increase the growth of the company by leaps and bounds

Learning:

1. Undergo training in "Leadership and Organisational Behaviour" can work wonders in the professional and personal journey of an individual's growth.
2. The value of making the right decisions at the right time is important.

3. Know that you are the master of your own destiny. To be brave, bold and decisive is the key to success.

4. Always do something for the community and not just for profit, as evidenced by the foundation of the Solan Paanch Parmeshwar Temple.

5. What is meant to come to you will come to you, but not without hard work and effort from your end.

Chapter defining quote:

"Hard work and discipline are essential for success. While hard work can compensate for lack of intelligence to some extent, discipline is non-negotiable."

Section 10
Acknowledgements and Tributes

"Proving time and time again that a friend in need is a friend indeed."

Part I: A Tribute to a Cherished Friend

Unwavering Friendship of Mr. GK Vithal and His Family

I met Mr. Girish Kumar Vithal in 1983 at his laboratory at the Heavy Water Plant in Kota, Rajasthan. After a lot of convincing him and some other laboratory personnel working under him, he, in turn, convinced his plant manager to give a chance to an Indian product as the manufacturer, yours truly, is a really good Engineer with a Ph.D. in Chromatography from the UK.

He placed an order for one Gas Chromatograph with a recorder. We supplied and commissioned the same in his laboratory. I stayed at their guest house for about one week to train their staff for operation and routine maintenance.

We supplied the equipment as per order. They did not place the order for accessories required for use after installation (known as consumables). At Mr. Vithal's request, I left all the spares and consumables that I had with me. He treated me like any scientist treats another scientist. He organised accommodation at the Guest House, transportation facility to and from the plant, meals, etc., during my stay in his laboratory. On the last day, which was a Sunday, he invited me to his house for breakfast and introduced me to his wife, Mrs. Suneeta Vithal, daughter Mahima and his elderly mother.

I was given exceptionally good treatment and served a grand Punjabi breakfast. Mr. Vithal's mother told me, "Whenever you come to Kota, please take all meals at my house as it is only a five-minute walk from the Guest House."

Since this was our first supply to Heavy Water Plants, I used to visit every two to three months to monitor the health of the instrument and also the confidence of the users in our equipment, as earlier, they only had all imported/ branded chromatographical instruments. Each time, Mr. Vithal persuaded me to leave all the spares and consumables that I had in my installation/ service kit free of charge as it would take a very long time for them to process their requirements through the official channel.

I always gave him whatever consumables he demanded for the effective use of the analyser. From Kota, he moved to Heavy Water Board Mumbai as General Manager and directly or indirectly made us do R&D and develop a Tailor-made Indigenous Analyser. We learned a lot from him and with his help, we developed many GC attachments and also produced an indigenous Online Gas Analyser to meet his analytical requirements on a very crucial project.

That's how we became very good friends.

In 2012, my elder daughter-in-law, Lovely, suffered from a stroke and she was advised by the doctors in Baroda to be shifted to Hinduja hospital in Mumbai immediately. Around 11 o'clock in the night, I called Mr. Vithal and told him that we would be reaching Mumbai the following morning at 8:30 am by Rajdhani Express in a special 1st AC Coach.

I also asked him to organise an ambulance from Hinduja hospital as she was unconscious and had lost control over her faculties. Mr. Vithal organised everything, much more than our expectations and wishes and Lovely was admitted to Hinduja hospital. After admitting her, I and my wife along with Lovely relatives went to Bhabha Atomic Research Centre (BARC) Colony at Anushakti Nagar, Chembur where one scientist friend of mine from BARC offered me his completely furnished flat close to Mr. Vithal's flat. There were 7-8 people who were staying in that flat. Mr. & Mrs. Vithal came in the evening and insistingly took me and Kiran to their flat.

I asserted that we should stay along with Lovely's parents and our relatives who had accompanied her. In spite of our best persuasion, they shifted me and Kiran to their own master bedroom. Mr. Vithal shifted to the Pooja room and Mrs. Vithal shifted into their daughter's room.

We used to go to the hospital every morning at 8 am and return around 7 pm. Mrs. Vithal was a lecturer in the Junior College at Anushakti Nagar and she left for college at 7:30 am daily after cooking and helping us with breakfast. This routine continued for 20 days.

Lovely recovered slowly. On many occasions, Mr. Vithal drove us to the hospital to meet her. He always came from the office around 9 pm when I was fast asleep. He would never disturb us then. Once Lovely recovered fully and was discharged and we were to leave for Baroda the next morning, Mr. Vithal woke me up around 9 pm and kept on chatting till midnight. Being the true friend he was, he wanted to ensure that everything was planned for departure from his home as well as the hospital perfectly in order to avoid any last-minute hassles. Throughout our stay in Mumbai, Mr. Vithal, Mrs. Vithal and dear Mahima Beti hosted us so well that we never missed our house in Baroda.

I'm sure that nobody can do what Mr. Vithal has done for Lovely, including myself. He's a unique personality. Throughout my roughly 40-year association with him, I found him to be the most honest and sincere person.

A Friend in Need is a Friend Indeed!

One highly impressive quality of Mr. Vithal is his tremendous patience with a very positive attitude. He is very practical and accepts every situation as it is and handles it with full dedication. He doesn't mind taking help from any one whose guidance may be useful to handle the situation. The most prominent example is the case of his only daughter, beloved Mahima.

She was born with an auto-immune, non-curable disease called Lupus. They learned about it when Mahima was at the 9th standard in Mumbai. Though it was really shocking for both parents, Mr. Vithal soon realised the severity of the disease and motivated Mrs. Vithal and Mahima to accept it boldly and go for its treatment/ prevention through all the possible means. His attitude gave Mahima the strength to boldly face the consequences and she kept on putting her best in her academics. She finally completed her B.E. in Electrical Engineering with distinction and was placed as an R&D Engineer at Schneider Electric, Bengaluru. In 2017, Mahima was to be put on dialysis and Mrs. Vithal donated her kidney to her. What a remarkable step by Mrs. Vithal!

With full support from her parents, Mahima completed her MBA with 11th rank at Navrachna University, Baroda. Unfortunately, during COVID-19, her kidney was rejected. Mahima's medical facilities after attaining 25 years of age were promptly extended by the Director Bhabha Atomic Research Centre, though unfortunately, she passed away on 26th May 2022. Her medical expenses would be around Rs. 1 crore, which was fully paid for by BARC. This was the reward of their honesty and sincerity.

These incidents illustrate the character, behaviour, attitude and sacrifice of the power of an Outstanding Scientist and his family. As I have mentioned earlier in this book, his mother was very fond of me and seeing our chemistry, it was her desire that Vithal's family should shift to Baroda after retirement. It was her inner feelings that his son and his family would be in a very safe environment where Dr. Shingari resides.

Lastly, Mr. Vithal and his family are a part of my family and he respects me as his elder brother as well as a fellow Scientist. He's staying in a flat jointly selected by both families in Baroda since August 2015.

I'm forever grateful for their friendship and I wish both of them a healthy, happy and peaceful life ahead!

Part II: Gratitude for Medical Doctors

After my cardiovascular problems occurred in Pahalgam on 22nd Oct. 1977, I moved to Varanasi and shown to the Cardiologist in the Medical College cum Hospital of BHU and there the doctors told me it was a nature's warning and that I should change my lifestyle and must slow down.

On reaching Baroda, I contacted Dr. Kamal Pathak, H.O.D of Dept. of Medicine and Dean of SSG Hospital and College through Late Ishwar Bhai Haribhakti and discussed the findings of BHU doctors. After hearing about my problems, he took me to Dr. Kantaben Patel, who was In-charge of the ICU and the Professor of Medicine and told us that she was better than him. Kantaben admitted me to the ICU for three days, observed all parameters and confirmed the findings of the BHU doctors with suggestions for a healthy diet and lifestyle also prescribed me medicine for high B.P. Since 1977 till date, she has been my Medical Consultant.

Through Dr. Kantaben, I met Dr. Atul Saxena, Head Surgery 'B Unit' Govt. Medical College for my Surgical problems and we became very good family friends. His wife, Dr. Mita Saxena, is in her Physiotherapy Clinic and takes care of any associated problems. Through Dr. Atul Saxena, I came in contact with Dr. Archana Desai, H.O.D of E.N.T., SSG Medical Hospital. Her husband, Dr. Anupam Desai, is having his own hospital and Archana joined him after retirement. They are taking care of all our E.N.T. problems.

The present H.O.D of Surgery is Dr. Adeesh Jain, who has taken charge after Dr. Saxena's retirement and is also our very good family friend. Dr. Saxena joined Parul University Medical College as H.O.D, Surgery.

Professor Dr. Vishwanath Chawli, Orthopedics Dept. SSG Hospital and Mrs. Dr. Krishna Chawli having her own clinic are also our very good well-wishers and family friends.

Dr. Arvind Iyer, Physician cum Cardiologist of Subeksha Hospital, O.P. Road, respects me like his own father and any time of the day, he's available for us for any medical help required.

During my heart surgery, we developed a very close friendship with Dr. Parul Banker and her husband, Dr. Darshan Banker. Their son and daughter are specialists in different medical fields than the parents. We really appreciate the love and affection we receive from them!

Dr. Mrs. Minal Parikh is an eye surgeon and H.O.D of Haribhakti's Eye Hospital. She takes good care of our eyes and is a loveable character.

Dr. Poorav Desai is the Principal and most experienced doctor at the Homoeopathic College of Parul University Vadodara. He has cured me of Psoriasis (Auto-immune disease) and his treatment is still continuing in the 4th year. He considered me and my wife as his Uncle and Aunty and always gave free treatment whenever we required.

Dr. Mrs. Tashveen and her husband, Dr. Kamaljit Singh, have been our family friends for ages. Dr. Tashveen was my elder son Gaurav's Classmate and she is one of the best Dentists in Baroda.

Dr. Pradhan, the paediatrician, is another Doctor who has been treating my four grandchildren for the last 22 years without any professional charges from the very beginning. God knows why. He has a very pleasant personality.

It is worth mentioning that Dr. Shailesh Talati is the owner of one of the best gynaecology hospitals by the name of Eves Hospital in Baroda. My first granddaughter Mallika was born in his old hospital in 2001; he did not charge anything for the delivery at that time. We came to his hospital through the Commissioner of Income Tax (CIT). We thought he was very kind because of our contact with CIT. We gave Rs. 3,000/- for the welfare of his staff, who were very kind and nice. To our surprise, this trend of not charging continues for the delivery/consultation, etc., for the three grandchildren. He and his wife, Trupti, have been addressing me as Daddy. All the staff and Shailesh's family address me and treat me like a Daddy. Don't you think it is a blessing from God?

In Solan, Dr. Kailash Prashar and Dr. Lalita Prashar are very old family friends and they consider me as their elder bhaisaheb and responsible for our health and address medical problems when we are in Solan. Recently I have found two more Doctor friends from Shimla and they are Dr. Vinay Shankar and Dr. Mrs. Suman Shankar. Both have retired from Governemnt and educational jobs and have settled down in Solan. I am sure they will be like other Doctor friends.

Dr. Nisarg Mehta and Dr. Pranjali Mehta along with Dr. Jaimin Shah and Dr. Ami Shah have been a great support to us throughout. Very kind and helpful.

I and my entire family are very grateful and thankful to all the above-mentioned Doctors who have been helping us during our last 53 Years in Baroda and 31 Years in Solan!

May Almighty God Bless All of Them With Excellent Health and Happiness.

Part III: Acknowledgements and Admiration from Loved Ones and Colleagues

Mr. S Thyagarajan

Thank you for being my friend, Dr. Shingari!

Life is a wonderful journey of unexpected twists and turns and sometimes, it takes an unexpected wrong turn to put you in the right direction! This is how I would introduce my four-decade-long friendship. I remember the time we established SPINCO in 1981; we were a small, spirited team of highly passionate and enthusiastic people. With a plan to focus on a niche area in Biology, our goal was to make SPINCO unique as compared to other instrumentation companies. While quite a few customers were willing to guide us with their ideas to help us chart our path, we needed time to understand and move forward.

Hence, as an interim arrangement, to sustain and run the company, we decided to trade in laboratory equipment and unanimously agreed to include one advanced instrument in our offering that would not only showcase our expertise but also our commitment to support.

Given my knowledge and experience in Gas Chromatography (GC), GC was our choice of instrumentation. In the eighties, besides Toshniwal, there AIMIL (Associated instruments Manufacturers India, New Delhi), Netel (Mumbai), NuCon (New Delhi) and CIC (Chromatography and Instruments Company, Baroda), which were manufacturing GCs. I had met Dr. Shingari on a few previous occasions at customer sites and exchanged pleasantries, always being impressed with him as there was something that made him stand out from the others.

They say life can change in the blink of an eye, a chance meeting, a brief phone call, or a little thing that can alter one's life. This was exactly what happened on that hot Sunday afternoon in November 1981 when I phoned Dr. Shingari to inform him about the company. I had just started expressing my desire to distribute his GCs. He did not need much of an explanation and he conversed with me more like two old friends, catching up after a long time. His response was spontaneous; he said that SPINCO would start representing CIC in the south with immediate effect and he would extend every possible support from his side. What followed in the next week were brochures, quote templates with prices and a few leads that CIC was working on at that time. I knew all these customers already – Dr. Kalyanaraman of Flavours & Essence, Mysore; Mr. R. Vekatakuppaiya of CFTRI, Mysore; Mr. Sunil Vohra of Universal Oleoresins and Mr. Pratap Povani of Indo Cargo surveyors, Cochin. When I reached out to them with this new development, they were most pleased and felt this partnership would augur well for both of us.

Our success seemed guaranteed for multiple reasons. The first one was the personal brand that Dr. Shingari has built for himself - an expert in GC with a Ph.D. in Chromatography, from the UK. Secondly, this company was started by technocrats and Dr. (Mrs.) Shingari also has a doctorate from the BHU and is part of the management team. The last yet most compelling reason was that the company focused mostly on GC, unlike other companies, which had a large range of product offerings. Moreover, Dr. Shingari had built a reputation for his GC already, which I was aware of. In his possession were a bunch of valuable testimonials from various national laboratories, each one praising the performance of CIC GC in comparison to other International brands. These testimonials weaved magic, leaving the customers spellbound.

We got started, promoting the GC of CIC with a spiral-bound value proposition to the customer, complete with a cover letter detailing the background of Dr. Shingari and explaining why CIC should be the only preferred choice, armed with 100 such copies, in addition to the brochures and 50+ testimonials we set out. Having assured Dr. Shingari of phenomenal success for his GCs, we worked very hard, posting the spiral-bound quotation to 50 customers in the very first week. Those were the days of the typewriter and this format caught the attention of our customers as the secretarial staff had only to type the name of the customer on the already printed quotation booklet!

I vividly recollect the first order that came from a chemistry Professor from the Indian Institute of Technology, Madras. While preparing the order sheet, he asked me how many months it would take for the delivery. My reply seemed to stump him as I informed him that the installation would be completed before the end of the week.

All this confidence stemmed from the fact that Dr. Shingari had told me earlier that CIC had a stock of GCs and he would be able to send the instrument through the bi-weekly Navjeevan Express with a messenger immediately upon hearing from us. Thus, even before we received the order from the IIT purchase department, we received the consignment at Madras. The IIT Professors had not seen this kind of speedy service; hence, this installation was pivotal in securing more future orders.

Subsequently, a few months later, after having supplied a few GCs, I had an opportunity to meet Dr. Shingari at the Central Pollution Control Board in Bangalore. We were very happy to see each other in a very different role. Explaining our promotional activities for his GC, I shared a copy of our spiral-bound quotation booklet and he was highly impressed with our approach of promoting his GC. We both extensively travelled to Bangalore, Mysore, & Cochin, meeting customers and closing orders and I admired the way Dr. Shingari always showed keen interest in customers, which helped him build a personal rapport with them, who then became CIC's spokesperson in the industry.

When I visited his factory in Baroda, he introduced me as a marketing wizard to his team and asked me to address his staff on the nuance of sales and marketing. He shared with me all his future plans and personal goals. I stayed at his home during this visit and this later became my routine for years whenever I visited Baroda. I was particularly overwhelmed by the kindness, warmth and hospitality with which Dr. Shingaris took care of me.

In 1982, the Government of India constituted the National Biotechnology Board as a prelude to creating a separate Department of Biotechnology. This was the kind of opportunity that SPINCO had been waiting for and we began focusing on foreign instruments for upstream and downstream processing. We started using the double helix DNA structure with a slogan – 'SPINCO, the one-stop source for all instrumentation for Biotechnology.' By then, SPINCO had also developed a unique business model, making our friends as partners in different regions. When I approached Dr. Shingari's help to cover the important Gujarat market, he agreed spontaneously despite his other commitments. He played a major role in SPINCO getting orders for Fermentor, HPLC,

Transilluminator, Incubator Shakers, Ultra-low freezers, etc. Those were our formative years and we had to prove ourselves to our global principals through our success all over India. The support of Dr. Shingari at the right time bolstered our image as a leader in our chosen market, 'Biotechnology.'

It was during one of my visits to MS University of Baroda when I was asked to give a lecture on HPLC to students the very next day by Prof. C. V. Ramakrishnan, the Head of the Biochemistry Department (his son, Dr. Venki Ramakrishnan got the Nobel prize in Chemistry in 2009). I could not refuse, but I was hesitant and tensed as I neither had any slides nor a script ready. I was supposed to address a gallery full of students explaining on the blackboard and answering the questions from the Ph.D. scholars. Dr. Shingari encouraged me, infused confidence in me and gave me books on Chromatography to read and prepare overnight. He assured me that he would be sitting in the front row and would intervene anytime if required to help me. The lecture was very well received and this incident instilled in me the confidence to make future presentations on different topics in the future.

My association with Dr. Shingari is more than just a friendship. Besides the personal rapport based on matching frequencies and passion, we have genuine admiration and trust for each other. I recall, after four decades with pure pleasure, his courtesy, right from picking me up at the airport, fixing appointments, facilitating my visit to the customers and ensuring every visit of mine was successful. I have vivid memories of my morning tea (in my case, it was coffee) with him every day on the lawn in front of his house, discussing the day's plan, playing with his children Gaurav and Amar, family lunch and dinner. Dr. (Mrs.) Shingari was a great host, making me feel most comfortable understanding my shyness at not being proficient in Hindi and that I was not accustomed to eating chapatti and dal, day in and day out, for lunch and dinner.

Dr. Shingari had high regard for my wife, Latha. He used to appreciate her in superlative terms whenever he visited our home in Chennai, crediting her for my success and that of SPINCO. I still remember that instance when he called me out of the blue, asking me to talk to my wife first! Apparently, he was in touch with a family in Chennai, an alliance for his son, Amar and he wanted Latha to visit the family and talk to the girl. He opined that if Latha was satisfied and approved the girl and her family for Amar, he would come with his family to finalise the wedding arrangements. We argued with him that finalising an alliance should be entirely Dr. Shingaris' and Amar's call. But he stood his ground as he had so much confidence in Latha.

Of course, Latha and I went to meet the Mehra family. Poonam had just returned from college, with whom Latha then had a long chat. Undoubtedly, Poonam's graciousness pleased Latha and the recommendation was made to Dr. Shingari in the evening. In due course, Dr. Shingari visited Chennai to finalise the marriage arrangements with Mehra who then visited Baroda and performed the "Roka Ceremony." After this, Mr. Mehra and his family, including Poonam, visited Baroda and the engagement took place at Dr. Shingari's residence. All this happened on the recommendation of my late wife, Latha. The marriage took place at Dr. Shingari's residence, followed by the reception. Latha and I were present on both happy occasions at Baroda.

Abounding in kindness, empathy, compassion and humility, Dr. Shingari is a great human being. An exceptionally good entrepreneur with a rare blend of science, engineering and creativity, his leadership qualities, particularly his self-confidence and his love to take chances, have made him highly successful in all his ventures.

There are friends, there is family and then there are friends who become family! I wish Dr. Mahender Kumar Shingari and Dr. (Mrs.) Kiran Shingari, good health, long life, happiness, joy and prosperity!

Dr. V Shrinet

He is an eminent scientist with a Ph.D. in Physics from BHU. He is the Deputy Director at ERDA and a Senior Scientist at CSIRO, Melbourne and GE – R&D in the USA. He has authored 150 Research papers, received two National Awards, one State

Award and the International WIPO Gold Medal Award and has secured fourteen patents.

It is an honour and great pleasure for me to express my gratitude to Dr. Shingari. At the outset, let me take the liberty to introduce myself. I, Dr. V Shrinet, born and brought up in a remote village in Uttar Pradesh, did Ph.D. in Physics from Banaras Hindu University in 1985. I arrived in Vadodara by train at 5 am on 7th October 1985 to join scientist B position in (ERDA) Electrical Research and Development Association, Vadodara.

I dropped my baggage at the railway station's clock room. I had a lot of concerns at that time as no one knew me in Gujarat. However, one of my dear colleagues and very close friends, Dr. Sagina, had an acquaintance with Shri Vipin Vohra, who was an accountant at CIC. A very close friend of mine from BHU, Dr. Sagina, gave me an introductory letter for Vipin Ji. After a great hesitance, I met Vipin Ji in his office at CIC, Makarpura, Vadodara, at about 10 am on 7th October 1985. He was happy to see me and the letter from Dr. Sagina. Vohra ji took me to his boss, Dr. M.K. Shingari. I was welcomed by Dr. Shingari during our first meeting. Then, Vipin Ji dropped me at ERDA on his scooter. Later, he also came to receive me from the ERDA gate at 6 pm on the same day. By the evening, to my pleasant surprise, Dr. Shingari had arranged everything that I was worried about, such as how to pick up my luggage, where I would stay, etc. Immediately, he asked his driver to go to the railway station to pick up baggage. Vohra ji accompanied me to the railway station and the letter dropped me in his factory guesthouse. Later, he rented his own house to me for years. Since then, Dr. Shingari has always treated me like a family member and took all care. Considering my background at UP, I did not expect that an unknown person would take such great care and hospitality. Perhaps this is the main reason I could not leave Vadodara in spite of getting various excellent opportunities at General Electric, Bengaluru CSIRO, Melbourne, etc.

I have very high regard for Dr. Shingari, who is growing with time. A person with a tough childhood goes to complete a Doctorate in Chemical Engineering from the UK. He could have got an excellent job anywhere in the globe, but he chose his motherland. He could have become a professor like his father-in-law, who was H.O.D of Dept. of Political Science at BHU and Dr. Shingari could have got a position in any prestigious Indian university, but as his nature to face challenges head-on, he chose the difficult path of manufacturing. Manufacturing infrastructure at that time was not friendly, unlike now. He started manufacturing one of the very complicated, delicate and sophisticated analytical instruments, i.e., the Gas Chromatograph. He always followed very tough routines for himself, such as waking up early (around 4 A.M.) irrespective of the weather and continuously working late. I found him very benevolent (not to me alone but to whoever comes to his contact), professional, passionate leader, caring guardian and man of commitment; anyone can vouch for his words. The only limitation I found is that he is very disciplined, sincere and honest and expects similar qualities from an ordinary person like me.

As someone who has witnessed firsthand Dr. Shingari's unwavering pursuit of excellence, I am deeply inspired by his dedication and vision. His high expectations encourage others to strive for greatness, making him not just a mentor but a true role model. I am forever grateful for his guidance and consider him a guardian angel in my life, guiding me towards success and fulfilment.

I have never met an angel in my life, but I am confident that the angel must be like Dr. Shingari. He is a role model for our generation. I will always be indebted to him.

Mr. Devendra Prakash Gupta

He was the Chief Engineer (Rtd.) at Delhi Vidyut Board, Govt. of Delhi. This tribute is from him and his wife, Mrs. Sulakshana Gupta, Associate Professor, Political Science (Rtd.), university of Delhi.

Mahender, as we fondly remember him from our formative years, has always been the epitome of joviality, consistently keeping our spirits high and ensuring we enjoy life regardless of the prevailing circumstances. One outstanding trait that has defined him is his unwavering determination to pursue his goals with relentless perseverance, undeterred by any challenges or obstacles that may come his way. This inherent quality has been instrumental in his remarkable achievements, including earning his Doctorate in Chemical Engineering from the UK and establishing a successful Chromatography company from the ground up, transforming it into one of the most reputable corporate entities in India.

Mahender has been an early riser since childhood, waking up around 3 to 4 A.M. every day without fail. This habit persisted from his student days through adulthood. He believes in making important decisions during these early hours. He used to visit our house promptly at 5 A.M., a routine my mother cherished.

This practice continues today, as early mornings offer convenient transportation options and a serene environment, saving time and providing a fresh start to the day. During his early business days, Mahender travelled extensively, spending nights travelling and days dedicated to work. Despite my repeated advice to slow down, he remained obstinate. I often warned him, saying, "one day, I will be bringing your dead body home from the train." Ignoring my concerns, he continued his hectic schedule, leading to his first heart attack in Pahalgam in 1977. Though he briefly slowed down afterwards, he eventually returned to his old routine. Despite being a heart patient, having undergone two surgeries and receiving four stents, he remains unchanged in his habits.

Even at the outset of his married life, Mahender exemplified leadership and forward-thinking by opting for a simple ceremony at the Arya Samaj Mandir in Delhi, setting a commendable example for the youth of his time. Despite his reputation as a strict disciplinarian in ordinary circumstances, he is known to be a devoted husband, a loving father and a dependable friend in times of need. His unwavering commitment to his family and friends is a testament to his character & integrity.

Dr. Malti Sarin

Retired from the National Health Services of the United Kingdom after working for 60 years.

I have known Mahender for the past 55 years, as he is the husband of my younger sister, Kiran. Throughout this time, he has consistently presented himself as an epitome of elegance, often seen dressed like an English gentleman, complete with a tie or scarf around his neck.

Remarkably, despite being in his 80s, he maintains a youthful appearance and exudes vitality. His dedication to maintaining a polished appearance is commendable and adds to his overall demeanour. Mahender's academic achievements are equally impressive. He pursued and completed his M.Sc. and Ph.D. in Chemical Engineering without any external assistance, securing scholarships from the University of Wales to support his studies, which continued until the completion of his education. His academic journey is a testament to his intellect, determination and self-reliance qualities that have been evident throughout his life.

Throughout my acquaintance with Mahender, his traits of punctuality, diligence, foresight and unwavering motivation have been apparent. These qualities have been instrumental in propelling him towards success and have played a significant role in shaping his accomplishments. It is evident that his dedication and hard work have been key factors in shaping his life's trajectory.

As Mahender continues his journey through life, I extend my heartfelt blessings and wishes for his continued well-being and fulfilment. May he always find success and contentment in all his endeavours and may any remaining desires he harbours be fulfilled by the grace of God. By the way, I was born on 17th December 1941, whereas Mahender was born on 1st November 1941. He is almost one-month older than me.

Rajesh Shah (BE Electronics MSU)

On the journey of an Ek Refugee Scientist, the eye-catching reality of a person who changed the world through hard work and intelligence is revealed.

"There is time to be born, time to be grown and time to die." Dr. Shingari, Our mentor, is a perfect example to prove that "Destiny can be changed by firm determination and hard work."

Dr. Mahender Shingari is my friend, Philosopher and Guide. "This is how I Admire you to perceive you & this is how I look out for & find you." This is not only for us but also for our ex-employees who found Industrial space to set-up an ancillary unit with financial and work support from his company. He is the one who Offered a beautiful space to start our own company on

15th Aug 1985. My partner, Mr. Ramesh Manwani and I went to meet Dr. Shingari at his residence, DR. and DR., with our request to give us a small space to start our company. Dr. Shingari told us that the whole 3-storey building opposite my residence is lying vacant; you go and select the suitable space. We went and found that on the second floor one flat consisting of three rooms with an area of about 900sq. Ft. was more than adequate for us to start our business. We selected the top floor with the intention that rent would be minimal, being on top.

We came back and told Dr. Shingari that flat no. One on the second floor is suitable for us. On inquiring we wanted to know the rent payable every month. We were very surprised by his answer that you are occupying and starting your company. "You can pay the rent whatever you feel appropriate, as and when you are able to make the payment, or after you start earning." Since we were on top of the building, we decided to give the name- "Cliff Electronics." Further, he helped us to give 1st order with advance to Design and Development of process control instruments required for his GC.

This Gentleman became our landlord and Godfather who always stood by the US for anything "Wish at Command" and associated in every aspect of our life. We could not have achieved success without him. His Joyful & Kind Nature enlightens our path to our life with good health & Peaceful mind, which is essential for the growth of anybody.

We are proud to be "Part & Partial" of the Shingari family, which taught us to be KIND and show empathy to others. "If you do good to others, Nature will do good to YOU." Simple life, low-profile and humbleness are the motos of life.

Ramesh Manwani

It is my privilege and great pleasure to pen down a few words for Dr. M.K. Shingari for his autobiography "Ek Refugee Scientist." We always remember Dr. Shingari as Dr. Saheb, who is, fortunately, our 1st landlord. I have known him since 1975, when I contacted him for my vocational training for 30 days at his company, CIC. Upon joining my training, Dr. Shingari took me to his workshop and told me to sit there and make the drawings of all the sub-assemblies being fabricated there.

We have some sweet memories of visiting Dr. Shingari's house first time in the year 1985. When I told Rajesh Shah that you pay when you earn. He could not believe me at all. I am in partnership with Rajesh Shah and name of my company is "Cliff Electronics." We started our company Cliff Electronics from top of the building and so name Cliff Electronics was justified. Our terms of payment were to pay rent after we earned from business.

Dr. Saheb gave us 1st order in advance (without our asking) and later on, we became the design and manufacturing company of CIC, developing products for them. We have never looked back to date. Dr. Shingari is our family friend, mentor and role model. He taught us punctuality, honesty, sincerity and a strict, disciplined life.

It is not out of place to mention that we started our company with Rs. 10,000 as our capital and today, we have grown into two midsized companies, Cliff Electronics and Deluxe Electronics. Venture capital (VC) and start-up terms are used very frequently by the present Government, but Dr. Saheb has always supported us financially and otherwise and these thoughts are always in our minds. It is a really great journey to have a friend like Dr. Saheb, as we affectionately call him and we are deeply obliged to God for giving us an opportunity to get to know a person like Dr. M.K. Shingari.

Mr. G.K. Vithal

Outstanding Scientist, Ex-GM (Process chemistry & Analytical Laboratory), Heavy Water Board, Department of Atomic Energy. Recipient of 7 DAE Group Achievement Awards.

We feel very proud to write about a unique and rare personality Dr. M.K. Shingari, 15 years elder to us, who in fact is now our friend, philosopher and guide in all walks of our life.

Dr. Shingari met me for the first time somewhere around 1983 in my office at Rawatbhata, Kota, Rajasthan. I was in-charge of (the Process Chemistry & Analytical Laboratory) Heavy Water Plant, an Industrial unit of the Department of Atomic Energy (DAE). He met me to introduce his indigenous Laboratory

Gas Chromatographs (GC) as he was a regular supplier of Online GC to Rajasthan Atomic Power Station, next door to us and another industrial unit of DAE. He also had an annual maintenance contract. He briefed me about his Ph.D. work on separation techniques and the design of a prototype production scale GC in the UK. He also gave me two books authored by him, viz. "Handbook on Chromatography for Chemists and Engineers," "Atlas of Chromatograms by Gas Chromatography." He also gave me one book edited by Prof. Sukhmar Maiti, H.O.D of Material Science, IIT Kharagpur, where Dr. Shingari contributed two major chapters on the Chromatography of Polymers, Petroleum and Petrochemicals. This book is based on the papers presented at the Symposium and Workshop held at the Indian Association of Science, Calcutta, December 26-28, 1978.

Knowing the relevant background on GC as well as designing & maintaining Online GC for Nuclear Reactors, I decided to buy one laboratory model for the analysis of impurities in Nitrogen and Hydrogen Sulphide Gases being produced and utilised at our plant. The imported GC, which was already available in the lab, had embargo issues on spare procurement and maintenance issues due to frequent changes of Indian representatives. Though I was cautioned by my Works Manager about the quality of Indian-made products and services to be provided by Indian Manufacturers, seeing the background and confidence of Dr. Shingari, I persuaded the Works Manager to give a chance to indigenous products.

That was the beginning. Then, after placing an order, GC was satisfactorily commissioned by Dr. Shingari and his team well before the schedule. In fact, he left a few consumables with me, though these were not ordered. He explained that he is always concerned about the convenience of his customers and just to avoid delays in case of any abnormalities, he keeps some important consumables with him. This sincerity, foresight and concern for the customer really impressed my work manager and me. Further, I found that in case of a breakdown of GC, Dr. Shingari will immediately send his maintenance person on a telephone call even though the purchase order for the same was placed later. That showed his commitment and confidence in customer integrity.

During subsequent interaction, we were discussing technical issues which required further R&D, I found that Dr. Shingari was always ready to accept the challenge and ultimately, he will provide amicable solution. The best example was development of Online Trace Analyser in Liquid Hydrogen. This scientific and positive attitude made me his fan and I don't know when customer - supplier relationship converted into lifelong friendship.

Dr. Shingari is a man of principle, discipline, commitment and at the same time, diplomacy, as he always gives very Frank advice when asked. He does not like to spend unnecessary time, even though he is an industrialist and he always remembers the struggles he faced in his childhood. Basically, he is a good human and helps genuinely needy persons outright through his trust. Interestingly, he is very social and nature-loving and always maintains a balance between professional and personal commitments. We also noted that he also gets angry when people don't finish tasks according to the jointly agreed schedule.

Now, he is more than an elder brother to us; he is always at our side whenever the situation arises. Not only him but also his entire family was grown by him and Dr. (Mrs.) Kiran Shingari is in a very disciplined but very cordial relationship to date. We always wonder how both of them manage a joint family, having two sons, daughters-in-law and four grandchildren in a present-day situation where everyone wants to live independently. Hats off to them and all their children who have so much regard for their parents and even their parents' friends.

In fact, we could understand Dr. Kiran Shingari when her elder daughter-in-law Lovely was admitted in Hinduja hospital and both of them stayed with us at Mumbai around 3 weeks. Both of them have excellent chemistry and are made for each other. We could then understand that toughness of Dr. Shingari and patience & politeness of Dr. Mrs. Shingari was the key to keep three generations together with harmony. Both of them are so informal that we always feel at ease with them.

Interestingly, my mother was also highly impressed by Dr. Shingari's behaviour, boldness and Frank opinions. She wanted him to take us to Baroda to settle after retirement. And see the destiny: though we have a flat in Mumbai, HER wish could be fulfilled and we feel very lucky and proud to have settled near him in Baroda since 2015.

We always find Dr. Shingari and their family at our side whenever the situation arises. They took complete responsibility for settling us at Baroda. At the time of my mother's death at Baroda in January 2021, we did not know how they arranged everything from the funeral to the final rituals. Similarly, whenever our beloved daughter, Ms. Mahima, was hospitalised, Dr. Shingari's daily morning call and frequent visits always boosted our and Mahima's morale. Unfortunately, when Mahima took her last breath, his entire family immediately rushed, consoled us and took over the charge of making all arrangements from the funeral to the last rituals.

We, in our life of nearly 70, have never met such a unique personality. We have no words to thank him except to pray to Almighty God to bless him with a long and healthy life and guide all of us.

Girish Vithal and Suneeta Vithal

Divesh Shingari

Dr. Shingari's Nephew settled in the USA after his BE in Electronics & M.S in Computer Science from the U.S.

There is a saying that "one father is more than a hundred schoolmasters." For me, my Tayaji is just like my second dad, always guiding and teaching me valuable life lessons. Tayaji has guided me in all aspects of my life whether it was education, work, intellectual or social aspects. He was a strict teacher, but that's what made me disciplined, punctual and accountable. I learned a lot from him by just observing how he lives his life. His exemplary life is a testament that anyone can do anything if they set their mind, heart and soul to it. Even at this age, he lives with the same vigour and passion as he did 20 years ago.

I am pretty sure you would have heard the very famous saying, "Give a man a fish and you feed him for a day; teach a man to fish and you feed him for a lifetime." Tayaji has lived by this principle his entire life. His philanthropic activities to promote and encourage education have empowered so many kids to follow their dreams, grow and contribute towards society.

I can rightly say that my success stands on a few pillars and the most crucial of them is my Tayaji. I didn't need to look outside for a role model. I just observed him and lived by his principles. There are a few life lessons from Tayaji that I live my life by and I hope they can add value to your life as well:

1. The only thing you can control is Hard Work. Just put your 100% and then have faith and hope for the best.
2. Always live below your means. There are two ways to get rich - either you earn more or save more. Since you can't always control your earnings, you can always save more.
3. There are two ways to get in front - by pushing yourself up or pulling others down. Always push yourself and grow yourself rather than worrying about others.

First Letter (Dated 1st November 2016)

Namaste Tayaji

This is token of thanks for all you have done for us. I don't have enough words to thank you because you have done so much for us. You taught us lessons of life starting from getting our admission in St. Lukes, which was definitely a life turning point in our life. That one decision changed our life made us what we are today. The peaceful environment and your continuous guidance was responsible to not let us deviate from our goal or indulge us in any misleading activities. You guided me through all the difficult phases, whether it was my 11th - 12th class or counseling or my college life. You were always there without any concern about your health. Sincere thanks for all.

I still remember that you taught us fundamentals of life in small and simple day to day example. Whenever we came to baroda you were always there with tayiji to support us. You used to scold us whenever we used to leave milk in our glasses, taught us the value of hard earned money. You taught us the basic table manners, how to deal with people effectively and efficiently. You were the one who molded our daily routine, taught us yoga, the art of planning and how to be confident.

You always tried to make us better in each and every aspect of life. You were responsible for creating a spark, a driving force to excel in each and every sphere of life whether it was studies, extracurricular, personal or social front.

Thanks a lot for always being there. I always pray that god bestow good health and you always be happy in whatever you do.

Yours loving
Davesh Shingari

With love from
Davesh

Second Letter (Dated 30th November 2021)

Dear Tayaji and Tayiji

A person is lucky to have supporting and loving parents, but I have been extremely fortunate and blessed to have you and tayaji as my secondary parents, who have guided me in each and every aspect of my life.

When we moved from Delhi to Solan, I was too young to fully understand the impact of this decision. But I feel extremely blessed to move there and get mentored by you and tayiji, whether it was as small as table decorum, getting up early, dealing with people or making big decisions of my life.

The biggest change for me was when you advised me to take competitive exam preparations seriously. You took the bold decision and told me that I need to leave school and go to Chandigarh for coaching. That was the defining moment of my career and I'm 100% indebted to you.

When I though of pursuing higher education, you supported me 100%. Without you it would not have been possible.

I still remember your saying "Hardwork is the only thing in your control, not luck." Some of those sayings have stuck by me and I have used them countless times as my guiding beacon.

I can't mention this enough, but no amount of words or actions will ever be enough for what all you have done for me. Thank you Tayaji and Tayiji from bottom of my heart.

With love from
Davesh

Nirmal Padda

An old friend from Swansea University, UK.

Akota, Mujmahuda, Vadodara-390 020.
T : +91 265 308 1234, F : +91 265 308 1235
E : rocv@royalorchidhotels.com
W : www.royalorchidhotels.com

14/1/14

Dear Mohinder jee
\+
family

It has been so nice to meet you after such a long time (45 yrs) since university days in Swansea (197--?) You have a nice family and all very well settled in life all because of your hard work in life. You are my mentor and Guru who taught me to work hard and then enjoy life with the family and friends.

May God bless you all and shower you with luck and prosperity in the future.

Hope to see you in Panjab in near future.

Love and Regards,

Nirmal Padda

BANGALORE : Hotel Royal Orchid • Hotel Ramada • Royal Orchid Suites • Royal Orchid Resort & Convention Centre • Royal Orchid Central
MYSORE : Royal Orchid Metropole • Royal Orchid Brindavan Garden HOSPET : Royal Orchid Central Kireeti GOA : Royal Orchid Beach Resort & Spa
AHMEDABAD : Royal Orchid Central PUNE : Royal Orchid Central • Royal Orchid Golden Suites MUSSOORIE : Royal Orchid Fort Resort
JAIPUR : Royal Orchid Central • Hotel Royal Orchid MUMBAI : Royal Orchid Central Grazai SHIMOGA : Royal Orchid Central

AND GROWING :
Surat, New Delhi, Bharuch, Noida, Tanzania

Love from the Shingari Family

Dr. Mrs. Kiran Shingari

Wife and Director CIC Pvt. Ltd. Vadodara & Partner of Precision Scientific Instruments, Solan, Himachal Pradesh.

I am the wife and confidante of my husband, Dr. M.K. Shingari, a man of remarkable discipline, punctuality, hard work and exceptional intellect. His mind operates at a lightning-fast pace, allowing him to make swift, well-calculated decisions, both big and small, with an impressive accuracy rate of 95%. Despite his honesty, simplicity and occasional sternness, he excels as a devoted husband and father, always striving to uplift his family and those around him. In addition to his professional accomplishments, he is also the author of several technical books, showcasing his depth of knowledge and expertise in his field.

Throughout his life, my husband has demonstrated unwavering support and care for his family members, particularly his younger brother and his family. From a young age until the age of 77, he has shouldered the responsibility of caring for them, ensuring their well-being and happiness. He played an instrumental role in arranging the education and marriages of his brother's son and daughter, as well as financing his nephew's pursuit of a master's degree in the United States. His selflessness and generosity know no bounds, as he consistently puts the needs of his loved ones above his own.

My beloved husband is a man of integrity, self-respect and compassion, always striving for excellence and setting new goals for himself. His presence in my life has been transformative, shaping not only my outlook but also my personality. I consider myself incredibly fortunate to have Mahender by my side, who is a constant source of inspiration and love. I have been considering and telling him that, "You are my HERO, a real-life Hero and not a screen hero!"

Gaurav Shingari

Elder Son of Dr. Shingari

My Daddy, Dr. M.K. Shingari, is a highly disciplined and strict person. Though his lifestyle is very simple, He does not compromise on his principles. I want to narrate two incidents reflecting his real inner character. I was weak in math in 8th class. Shri Shah was my math teacher.

Dad requested that he take tuition to clear my fundamentals and teach me at home for 1 hour every day from 7 A.M. to 8 A.M.. He agreed, started teaching and came at the right time. On his 3rd day, he came late at 7:15 A.M., while on the 4th day, he came at 7:30 A.M.. Daddy was very angry and told him that when he is so indisciplined, he is not fit to teach a tender age child-like Gaurav.

He was immediately told not to come again and sent him back. We all including my mother was very much concerned as he was my class teacher. Daddy told us that he cannot dare to harm me. and if he tried to trouble me, Daddy would ensure that teacher would not be seen in the school again. Fortunately, nothing happened further as Shri Shah might have realised his mistake.

The other incident was when I was five years old. That was the time when there was a threat given by dad's rivals to kidnap his children. Our Principal, Dr. Prasad, told my father to keep me and Amar at home till our kidnapping threat was over. He bluntly told him that he had paid fees for a whole year and that He did not want his children to grow like cowards. We continued our school during those turbulent days. My father used to drop us off in the morning at the Principal's Office and also pick us up from his office 20 minutes prior to school time.

After my studies, Daddy gave me two years' experience in his friend's company, Kriton Welders, to realise the working conditions for employees. Initially, I was not very happy, but after joining Daddy's CIC, I realised his far-sightedness. This training helped me to understand the issues and attitudes of our company employees and bosses better. I have witnessed the remarkable growth and success of our companies from his real-life experiences during his long tenure of 52 years in business and 30 years in education in India and abroad. Therefore, Daddy has all the qualities of a HERO from the beginning. He is our REAL-LIFE HERO.

Gaurav Shingari

Mrs. Lovely Shingari

Gaurav Shingari's Wife & Elder Daughter-In-Law

Dr. M.K. Shingari's enthusiastic spirit and zest for life, coupled with his commitment to simplicity and discipline, set him apart in a league of his own. His unwavering dedication to maintaining a disciplined lifestyle, characterised by a balance of simplicity and efficiency, is truly admirable. From the moment the sun rises to its setting, he exudes a powerful and positive energy that never fails to impress those around him.

His ability to approach each day with vigour and determination is a testament to his inner strength and resilience. As his daughter-in-law, I feel a sense of pride and privilege to be associated with him. His exemplary qualities, including his unwavering discipline and positive outlook on life, serve as a source of inspiration to me and countless others. His consistent commitment to living a purposeful and disciplined life is a shining example for all of us to emulate.

Dr. Shingari's remarkable attitude towards life reaffirms the importance of maintaining a positive mindset and embracing simplicity in all aspects of our lives.

Lovely Shingari

Amar Shingari

Younger Son of Dr. Shingari

I am 49 years old and to date, I have not come across anybody as a tougher and stronger person like my Daddy Ji. He will never compromise on his principles and his philosophy at any cost. I am narrating two incidents that have changed my life. During my B.Sc. final year at MSU, I started smoking occasionally in my friend's circle. He was always busy with his work, going to the factory at 7:45 A.M. and returning most of the time at midnight. My mother came to know and warned me that if I didn't stop, she would complain to my Daddy and eventually, she complained to him.

Daddy gave me a warning that if I didn't stop smoking and meet friends who were not obedient and good boys, he would have to take strict action. After my graduation, I felt that I had achieved something very big in my life and again, I started mixing with my old friends who were smoking and were late coming. In response to my Mummy's complaint, he fired me left and right and told me that if I didn't improve, he would throw me out of the house. One night, I came home late in spite of his warning. He scolded me in front of my friends and I felt very bad and decided to leave the house. I told this to Mummy and she conveyed it to Daddy. Hearing this, he told me that Amar, with a B.Sc., had no value and nobody would recognise me. People respect me because I am Amar Shingari. I felt very bad and left the house the same evening.

At night, I could not arrange suitable accommodation for myself and ultimately spent the night at the Baroda Railway Platform. The police came at midnight and told me not to sleep there. I could not sleep that night, so I reviewed my dialogues with Daddy and decided to go back and apologise to him. I went back. Due to a really tough decision made by Daddy, I realised that life is not as simple as I imagined. The second incident was when we were staying in a 1 BHK C-type flat constructed by GIDC (for the company and its employees) to develop the industrial estate.

These houses were allotted to the factory owners for their workers. Subsequently, we shifted to a 2 BHK B-type flat, which was meant for factory owners. Both C-type tenements and B-type flats sold to us were of substandard in quality and 80-90% of houses were leaking very badly during the monsoon period. All the residents of the colony requested Daddy, being honest and tough, to take the appropriate action on their behalf. He told the regional manager to get the problem solved by rectifying the defects without any charges. No action took place even after the meeting and several reminders in writing. There used to be meetings in the late evenings, around 8 P.M. onwards. Daddy used to carry a stool with him to stand on the stool and regularly give assurance to the residents. One fine evening, he told all the residents to stop paying instalments due to GIDC towards the cost till they were fully repaired.

Eventually, the GIDC authority decided to repair and came to our house to repair our four houses. But Daddy did not allow them to start work at our house and told them in very clear words that they would have to start repairing C-type houses first and then come to B-type and lastly at our house. GIDC Contractor and their Engineer got the message that there was no choice except to be honest and start repairing the houses of poor workers. These incidents of my early life taught me a lesson and I started trying to follow in the footsteps of Daddy, who is very straightforward and uses simple & plain language which everybody can understand.

Also, Daddy is very strict and firm and does not compromise on his principles and ethics of efficient working. He taught all of us that at the end of the day of our work, we spend 5 minutes writing down what our output is and think whether it is reasonable and how to increase it further. He firmly believes in calculating his output per unit of time and puts his efforts into improving further. He rewards his efficient and disciplined working force.

I always pray to God to bless Daddy with a healthy life and guide us throughout.

Amar Shingari

Mrs. Poonam Shingari

Wife of Amar Shingari and Younger Daughter-in-Law

I don't have enough words to express how much I am grateful to you for welcoming me to your family with abundance of love and affection. You and my mother-in-law has been taking care of me and rest of the family from the day one. My father told me that after marriage I'm not your father anymore, Dr. and Mrs. Shingari are your parents hence forth.

Any problem in life, you consult them and not me. I am pleased to state that I have never contacted my father after marriage. I only speak to him when you transfer his call to me. You have been taking care of me, Amar, Arya & Anoushkaa.

You are our inspiration, our teacher, our Valuable Mentor, Guide & our Icon as well. We are fortunate to have you in our lives. You are also man of great integrity. Wishing you good health always.

Arya Shingari

Grandson

Ever since you became my grandfather and I your grandson, you've been dedicated to passing on your knowledge and wisdom to me without expecting anything in return, always ensuring my needs are met.

I will forever cherish the memories of waking up to your early morning calls of "Arya, wake-up!" and the playful pokes to get me out of bed. While others may remember you as the self-made man who built an empire, to me, you will always be the grandfather who loved all of us unconditionally. I am deeply grateful to you for the lessons you've taught me about discipline, honesty and hard work, as well as the values you've instilled in me and other family members.

I conclude, your legacy is not just the memories you have created with every one of us but the values you've instilled in us will always be remembered and followed.

Anoushkaa Shingari

Granddaughter (Pappo)

Dadu, you are the most dedicated, hard-working, disciplined, honest, straightforward and strictest person. I have never met or seen anybody like you in my life to date. I am very grateful to you for everything you have bestowed us with. Fighting with you is a part of my best memories. A single day doesn't go by where we don't fight during lunch and dinner time. Sometimes, I think that you are not able to digest food properly unless you fight with your "Pappo" and "Lachho." To conclude, I would like to say that we all respect and love you very much.

Your Pappo

Mallika Shingari

Granddaughter

In the realm of discipline and dedication, my grandfather stands as a model of unwavering commitment and meticulous planning. His devoted adherence to routine is nothing short of awe-inspiring, as he rises each day at the stroke

of 3-4 A.M. to embark on his morning exercise regimen and drink about 2-3L of hot water. A man of methodical precision, he approaches each task with meticulous attention to detail, exemplifying the virtues of organisation and planning in every aspect of his life.

His unwavering commitment to self-improvement and well-being serves as a testament to his unyielding spirit and serves as an inspiration to all who have the privilege of knowing him. I am proud to be his eldest granddaughter and I draw strength from his example as I pursue my studies at the University of Southern California (USC), USA, inspired by his unwavering dedication and tireless pursuit of excellence each and every day of his life reaching powerfully till today and still moving ahead with a lot of VIGOUR...

Shubhangini Shingari

Granddaughter (Lachho)

Handsome old man – no – I can't say that to Dadu. He is my handsome young man, suited, booted & scarfed up for everyday life. This was hard for me to say but I surely have a tough competition during our lunchtime discussions.

Wishing him all the best for his present book – An autobiography of Ek Scientist Refugee. He has already written two books. He is a writer, boss in the house as well as boss in the company.

Your Lachho

Anil Kumar Verma

Ex- Executive Director, ONGC

Dear MKS

You are like a giant tree
Of Practical Wisdom & knowledge.
May you live a healthy 100 years.
GET WELL SOON.

affectionately
Anil & Veena
Aug 2009.

Renu Sarin

Cousin of Dr. M.K. Shingari

I, Renu Sarin, Paternal Cousin of Dr. M.K. Shingari of Baroda, have known each other for the last 58 years. He used to come to our house regularly during summer vacation and we found him to be a very loveable all-rounder who took an interest in everything - support, music and movies. At present, he is the senior person in our family. My own daughter, Dr. Neha Sarin, went to Baroda to join the Home Science Dept. of M.S.U and came back with her Ph.D. She stayed with Bhaiya from the beginning till the end.

My son, who got his own company software, took a job from his company, but after 1 Year, he terminated his contract because of his poor service and Bhaiya was not satisfied with his work. In short, he's very strict and disciplined and he has no compromises with his work. I know one case in which he terminated the services of his younger brother, who was trained in the UK by his friend's company. Now you can see what character he is.

We all feel very proud and fully satisfied that some senior most person is with us to guide us, help us and take a firm stand in giving Frank and fair decision in our family disputes/problems.

We love him.

Mrs. Simanthini and Mr. Upendra Pandey,

Managing Director, GETCO, Govt. of Gujarat

We met Dr. Mahender Shingari ji first when we moved to Vadodara in 2021. He and his family make us feel at home in our new city. We fondly call him Uncleji and he has truly been a father figure to us all. We find Uncleji very wise and full of energy and enthusiasm. Perhaps his great yet simple hobbies, such as his love for plants and nature, affinity to old songs, etc., show his radiant energy. His pursuit of knowledge, despite having years of wisdom, makes him a truly inspirational figure. He is a self-made, strong person. He is himself a testimony to many important virtues in a successful person; the lessons we learn from him are: hard work has no substitute, happiness is dependent on self-discipline and honesty is the best policy. Whenever I get tired of overwork, I look at him for his extraordinary persuasiveness and motivation. It's true that a healthy mind lives in a healthy body.

Realising it truly, he leads a perfectly disciplined life; he starts his day early in the morning with exercise and walks to keep his mind agile throughout the day.

His family is a perfect example of three generations happily living together. Both Uncleji and Auntieji have instilled and preserved very good family values and morals in their family. They both have not only built their great business empire but have made their children very worthy of handling future challenges. We have seen Uncleji engaging everyone in very serious discussions and equally enjoying time with children, making him a charming person that everyone loves to be around. He is always very cheerful and has an abundant source of energy, which lights up a gathering or a party as soon as he enters. We are very grateful to have met such a caring, loving and helpful person. Uncleji, you will always hold a special place in our hearts.

His biography will show the 'way to success against all odds' to people of all ages. We wish him a happy, healthy and cheerful life. I am also waiting for another book on completing 100 years of a healthy life.

B.B. Chauhan

Ex Managing Director, GETCO, Govt. of Gujarat. Presently Executive Consultant to Reliance

It is my honour and privilege to have an opportunity to express my views about a dignitary having a strong mind, Caring nature, self-determination, the highest level of wisdom and much more none other than Dr. Mahender K Shingari ji. My over-decade-long association with Shingariji, which started professionally, has turned into family relations today. Personally, I admire such a great identity, Shingariji, who is leading amongst all but very few with whom I associate in my life.

After obtaining a doctorate from the UK in Engineering in those days (more than five decades) and coming to India to start my own venture, starting a company in Vadodara with limited resources and hard work, the company today have a self-recognition in high technology instruments used by major Indian Atomic / Defence / critical process industries which is a great contribution to our Nation INDIA. My family and I are grateful to Shingariji and his family members for treating us as their associates; truly, I have no hesitation in approaching him and any of his family members at any time. I must acknowledge the response I got so far and I am sure that I will get the same response in the future. We consider Shingariji as our father figure. Personally, even at this age of 82/83, he is very active, starting the day early in the morning with warming exercises and spending the whole day in his own way in the garden and in his own office. He is still very disciplined, active and full of energy. This, I can say, is only possible with simplicity and integrity. He is fully concerned not only for his family members but also for all associated with him, taking all the required care and always motivating others.

The biography of Dr. Shingariji shall definitely be prove as pathways for so many individuals to mold their profiles in today's highly competitive world and we wish great success to the endeavour undertaken by him. We pray almighty for good health to him and his family.

Col. Anil Kumar Sarin

Cousin of Dr. M.K.Shingari

I, Colonel Anil Kumar Sarin, a retired Army officer from the Indian Army, have known Dr. M.K. Shingari very well since childhood (since the age of 5 years). He is my cousin's brother, the son of my Bua Ji. We grew up together and he stayed with my parents in Aligarh until he completed high school in 1957. After that, he moved to Delhi to study further. Dr. Shingari has always been my favourite cousin and we share a deep understanding.

Dr. Shingari is known for his honesty and straightforwardness. He always speaks the truth without mincing words, regardless of whether it's what someone wants to hear or not. His decisions are always clear and he listens attentively to everyone's opinions, though he ultimately relies on his own judgement, which is independent and impartial. Convincing him to change his mind is a daunting task. Despite his tough exterior, I see Dr. Shingari as a complex individual. While he may appear to be a "hard nut to crack" on the outside, underneath, he is a very gentle, kind-hearted person who is incredibly supportive. My wife, Pinky Sarin, my daughter, Dr. Aditi Sarin and my son, Ditu, share the same opinion. Dr. Shingari holds the most senior position in our family and is regarded as a father-like figure.

45+ Years of Experienced Staff and their tributes

Respected Doctor Saheb,

I, Vipin Vohra, joined in 1981 after graduating from Banaras Hindu University. My cousin sister, Dr. Mrs. Kiran Shingari, attested to the disciplined nature of Dr. Shingari, emphasising punctuality and timely results. After retiring in 2018, I returned as a Senior Accounts Officer overseeing two accountants. We've imbibed discipline and hard work from our 83-year-old boss, who tirelessly works from morning till evening, even completing a Autobiography within two months.

I, Rakesh Shah, Vipin Vohra, Dayabhai Parmar - the following most senior staff have been working with you for the last 40 – 45 years in Chromatography and Instruments Company.

I, Rakesh Shah, began my career after graduating from M.S. University and intend to retire alongside you. My father, a Sales Tax Inspector, admired your integrity, leading to my training under your guidance for six months without pay. I joined the company as an Account Assistant in 1985. We're deeply grateful to Doctor Saheb for his guidance, which has enriched our professional and personal lives tremendously. Working under his mentorship has been invaluable to us.

Mr. Bipin Shah & Company has served as our chartered accountant since 1972 and his second generation is now continuing the legacy.

M/s. Haribhakti & Co., Chartered Accountants and Auditors, have been with us since 1972. Despite Mr. Ishwar Bhai Haribhakti's passing, we continue to work with his company's second generation.

Our boss does not believe in changing the people, but he will do his best to mould all of them to suit his requirements and temperament. We, the three longstanding staff, remain committed until Dr. Shingari Saheb retires, inspired by his belief that enjoyment in work ensures vitality. Our boss's philosophy keeps us energetic and dedicated, mirroring his own vitality.

Mrs. Shipra Desai

I want to share my experience working with Dr. Shingari Sir. When I joined CIC, I heard that Sir could be strict about work and discipline. Yes, he is strict about quality work and this made me a good technical professional.

Working with Sir taught me a lot. He didn't just give me work-related advice but also shared valuable life lessons. His guidance kept me motivated and helped me stay positive. He shared his own experiences, which gave me wisdom on how to handle similar situations in the future.

Moreover, Sir always appreciated my work and my attitude, which encouraged me to keep moving forward with a smile on my face. His encouragement meant a lot to me and kept me motivated in my work. I feel very happy and satisfied as I am associated with Sir!

Ms. Nida Amiri

To Dada Ji,

I hope this letter finds you well and smiling, as always!

I wanted to express my deepest gratitude for your guidance and support during the most crucial years of my life. Despite not being related by blood, you've treated me like your own granddaughter and I am incredibly grateful for your kindness. At the start of my internship under your guidance, I was nervous, having heard tales of your discipline from Arya. Yet, with time, I discovered there's more depth to you than meets the eye.

Working with you has been incredibly rewarding. Your wisdom has not only enriched my understanding of our work but also of life itself. Your encouragement has empowered me to strive for excellence in everything I do.

Your corrections come from a place of love, spurring me on to success. Your discipline, sincerity and caring nature inspire me daily. Your active engagement with life is truly admirable. Our talks about your friends and jokes about your ageless vitality have been a highlight for me.

Thank you for treating me like family, guiding me and encouraging me to be my best self. You're not just a mentor or friend but the most caring Dada Ji I could have wished for.

With heartfelt appreciation,

Nida.

Dr. Poorav Desai

Ph.D., Principal Homoeopathic College of Parul University, Baroda, Gujarat

Homoeopathy is a scientific mode of treatment that assists the body to heal itself. These days, many chronic, Auto-immune and Complex kind of diseases are prevailed in the society. Psoriasis is one of such kind and homoeopathy is the only surefire way to treat such illnesses. Dr. M. K. Shingari has had psoriasis for a long time and he choose homoeopathic treatment for the same.

As a doctor, I witnessed that in all successful case stories, A proper narratives of patient, meticulous explanation about all of their complaints and in accordance with, appropriate doctor's examination can determine the ideal course of treatment. Following to this regular consumption of medication and adhering to strict regimen in relation to complaints also play important role to ensure the complete recovery.

I am very much impressed with Dr. Shingari as he was taking all his medication for psoriasis religiously, very much punctual in follow ups and completely determined to beat this infamous illness with his positive attitude.

His such gesture truly set an example to a lot of such individuals who have given up on their chance to recover from such illnesses. My sincere gratitude to Dr. Shingari and all my best wishes to him to have a healthy and wonderful life ahead.

Mr. Sharabh Negi

IAS is an ex-district collector at Chamba, Kulu and many other districts in Himachal Pradesh

My first encounter with Dr. Shingari was in 1998 when he visited my office. At that time, I was the General Manager of the District Industries Centre in Solan. I remember my peon bringing me a visitor's card, and I was surprised to see Dr. M.K. Shingari, Managing Director, with impressive qualifications from London. Feeling guilty for making him wait, I quickly invited him in and made him comfortable.

I initially thought he had been misled into setting up an industry without understanding the bureaucratic challenges in India. I sympathetically asked who advised him to return to India and start a business. He acknowledged our working culture's challenges, and I promptly addressed his issue, which turned out to be routine and did not require a visit from such a senior figure. He was pleasantly surprised by the swift resolution, a rare experience for him in such offices.

Curious about why he returned to India, I learned more about him over subsequent meetings. This curiosity blossomed into a close friendship, extending to our families as well. I found Dr. Shingari to be friendly, trustworthy, and affectionate, like an elder brother. He also demonstrated punctuality, meticulous planning, diligence, and vision—qualities essential for a successful entrepreneur. These traits likely stem from his education and training in England.

Dr. Shingari is not only a leading entrepreneur and successful businessman in manufacturing precision scientific instruments, but also an outstanding father, good husband and caring family head. He maintains a harmonious family atmosphere and enjoys a reputation as a trustworthy and principled man. His friends and acquaintances see him as a guide and philosopher, always disciplined and modest.

His decision to return to India, despite having a bright future in England, reflects his Patriotism, self-esteem and strong principles. His life story, filled with struggles and triumphs, is inspiring. From humble beginnings in Lajpat Nagar, Delhi, to become a prestigious business figure in Vadodara, his journey is remarkable. I extend my congratulations and best wishes for his forthcoming autobiography, which I believe will inspire many others.

Mr. Kiritbhai Patel

A Renowned Developer of Vadodara, Since 1987 - 36 Projects completed in Gujarat and 2 Projects in Himachal Pradesh, 1 Project in Bangalore

I know Dr. M.K. Shingari for the past 25 years, ever since he purchased several residential plots in the Kanha – Kalali Project. This was our first transaction, and he made an exceptional offer to pay for all the plots immediately. He asked for a final price from the listed Rs. 220 per sq. ft. Since this was a unique offer early in my career, I asked him to write down his proposed price. He wrote Rs. 200 per sq. ft. with full payment within

24 hours. I accepted his offer, and to my surprise, he returned with the money within 24 hours. We completed the paperwork the same day, allotting all five plots to his family members. My partners and I found him to be straightforward, honest, and transparent.

After our first deal, Dr. Shingari invested in all my projects, including Planet Green, Satellite Green and other more projects. He has been one of the top investors, showing complete faith in me and my companies. Dr. Shingari often contacts me for advice on construction and long-term investments, and we have become good family friends.

Dr. Shingari is a man of principles, discipline, and high commitment. He always gives frank opinions and advice when asked. He is a good person, a good friend, and he helps needy people through his Charitable Trust.

At Dr. Shingari's request, I designed and constructed a five-storey building with seven flats, covered parking, and uncovered parking in Solan, Himachal Pradesh. This was my first project in the hills.

Now, Dr. Shingari is like an elder brother to me, and I draw a lot of inspiration from him. Even at his age, he remains active, disciplined, and performs his duties honorably. In all our projects, he supports me and others who are on the right path. He is a man of unwavering principles and integrity. I frequently give examples of his life and achievement to all my friends.

I have committed to throwing a grand party for Dr. Shingari and friends when he completes 100 years, which I am confident he will. To honor this commitment, I must live to host this celebration. This promise inspires me and reminds me of my dedication to him.

Section 11

Legacy and Concluding Advice

"In essence, success is not an elusive dream but a tangible reality attainable by those who heed the wisdom of the ages."

Part I: The Essence/Abstract of my Life's Work

In conclusion, my Autobiography narrates the remarkable journey of a 5-year-old boy who transformed into a proficient Engineer and Scientist after obtaining his Doctorate in Chemical Engineering from the UK. Emerging from humble beginnings exacerbated by the troubled events of 1947 partition of British India, my life story serves as a testament to the individual's resilience and the potency of unwavering determination. I conclude my Autobiography with insights gained, lessons learned and resolutions made, elucidating to readers the path to personal progress and fulfilment.

Born into a relatively affluent family, I encountered numerous trials and suffering from the tender age of five. As a refugee, I encountered countless hardships, compelled to abandon my roots and forge ahead in search of a more promising, purposeful and gratifying existence. Yet, through persistent effort, I successfully overcame serious difficulties encountered and charted a path to success in my homeland. With each obstacle overcome, I grew stronger and more resilient, drawing inspiration from the challenges that were coming my way and kept on pushing forward. I never looked backwards.

However, driven by an insatiable thirst for knowledge and an unwavering resolve to succeed, I pursued my education with relentless determination. Despite facing adversities and setbacks, I remained resolute in the pursuit of academic excellence, eventually garnering recognition for my intellect, diligence, patience, courage and faith in both myself and the Almighty.

Throughout my journey, I remained anchored by an unwavering commitment to my principles and values, steadfastly refusing to compromise my integrity, determination, positive outlook and aspirations. Despite achieving unprecedented success and acquiring wealth and societal acceptance beyond my wildest dreams, I remained grounded in humility and gratitude, never forgetting my modest beginnings and the trials that shaped me into the person I am today.

Reflecting on my life's journey, I am overwhelmed with gratitude for the opportunities offered to me and the support extended by mentors, colleagues, friends, family and the Government of India. Each individual and institution has played an integral role in shaping my destiny and aiding me in the pursuit of my goals and aspirations.

Ultimately, my Autobiography serves as a testament to the boundless potential of the human spirit and the transformative power of perseverance, resilience and determination.

It is a narrative of triumph over adversity, hope amidst despair and an unwavering determination to succeed against all odds.

Above all, it serves as a reminder that regardless of our humble beginnings or daunting challenges, Success is attainable with:

Faith, Self-confidence, Earnest Effort, Dedication and Noble Intentions.

Success doesn't just happen by luck. It comes from taking purposeful steps, being bold and sticking to wise advice. Famous sayings hold important lessons for anyone aiming for success. **"Where there is a will, there is a way"** sums up the importance of determination and never giving up. It shows that with strong determination, we can overcome any obstacle and reach our goals. Firmness in one's determination is essential for progress. By embracing the mantra of **"Come what may,"** individuals fortify their resolve and march forward undeterred by setbacks or uncertainties.

Drawing inspiration from the relentless determination of a river, which navigates around obstacles to reach its destination, we learn the invaluable lesson of perseverance and adaptability. Like the river, we must flow with unwavering resolve, charting our course through the trials and troubles of life.

Furthermore, the fact that the Sun gets temporarily covered by floating clouds teaches us to maintain optimism and resilience in the face of adversity. Hence, we too must continuously keep on trying through life's storms, knowing that every hardship is transient and will eventually pass away. By cultivating a positive outlook and unwavering faith, we can overcome any storm and emerge stronger on the other side.

Connecting with nature and surrounding oneself with greenery is another timeless principle for success. Nature has a remarkable ability to soothe the mind, rejuvenate the spirit and instill a sense of tranquillity. Amidst life's chaos and challenges, spending time in nature provides peace, comfort, clarity and renewed energy to confront obstacles with renewed vigour. By staying close to nature, we tap into its inherent wisdom and draw strength from its nurturing embrace. By staying close to the nature and following simplicity in life, one can manage good health. **Healthy mind stays in Healthy body.**

In essence, success is not an elusive dream but a tangible reality attainable by those who heed the wisdom of the ages. By embodying the principles of determination, resilience, optimism and connection with nature, individuals can overcome adversity.

Part II: The Peaks and Troughs of Life, Presented as Invaluable Lessons

Managerial success encompasses not only efficiency but also effectiveness. Efficiency entails completing tasks in a timely manner, whereas effectiveness involves executing tasks correctly within the given timeframe. **A manager who lacks punctuality and discipline cannot expect to lead a team of punctual and disciplined employees effectively**. The leader or manager must set an example by embodying punctuality, discipline and enthusiasm to cultivate a similar mind set within the team.

Positive motivation plays a crucial role in fostering a conducive environment for creativity and quality output among employees. It is imperative to create an organisational climate where employees are encouraged to work smarter, not just harder. While efficiency is important, it is equally essential to prioritise tasks based on their importance and impact. Delegating power to subordinates should be based on their character, sincerity, loyalty, knowledge, expertise and skills.

It is highly recommended to manage staff through guiding and demonstration techniques in today's world. Sir Harvey Jones, who successfully turned around Imperial Chemical Industries (ICI) in the UK, emphasised the importance of **Effective Leadership in Organisational Transformation**. According to Sir Harvey, even the best strategy and intentions cannot yield results unless everyone in the organisation understands the goals and contributes their best efforts to achieve them.

Based on 52 years of my Industrial experience in:

- Travelling all over the world
- Dealing with Multinational Companies
- Dealing with Government Establishments
- Industrial Manufacturing
- Marketing
- Management of workforce

I strongly recommend that the following **TEN COMMANDMENTS** shall essentially be incorporated into an individual's character for improving both Professional and Personal life:

1. **Planning :** Before execution of any work, meticulous planning is very important to avoid surprises and subsequent delays during the execution.

2. **Execution :** Time management and strict vigilance of work being executed will lead to proper and timely completion of the work.

3. **Team Development :** Bringing the workforce together as a team and maintaining a positive and enthusiastic attitude towards them brings the best output from an individual. Never underestimate the power of enthusiasm. Team formation is essential for growth and leaders for tomorrow. Also, one should be humble and quick to admit mistakes and avoid criticism.

4. **Hard work and Discipline :** Hard work is the most important quality in an individual to successfully achieve it's goals. Discipline and Punctuality as a habit enhance the working environment making the cordial relations among the team leaders and members.

   Setting an example by being punctual and disciplined in all endeavours by the team leader motivates the team. It is to be remembered that one should Work smarter and not only harder.

5. **Sincerity and Loyalty:** Loyalty to the organisation by every individual and following the instructions very sincerely is the most essential characteristic of an individual for a happy and comfortable life.

6. **Clear Communication:** Clearly communicate Organisational Vision and Mission to all team members will enhance the quality of work output. Ensure that your goals are clear, challenging and achievable.

   Additionally transparent communication with team members at every stage is also very important for continual growth of the Organisation.

7. **Accountability through Effective Delegation:** Delegate tasks based on an individual's Strengths and Capabilities and monitor their performance and accountability.

8. **Continual Improvement:** A wise man makes more opportunities than he finds. As you reach your goals, set new ones. This is how you can grow and become more Powerful. Embrace a mind set of continuous learning and growth, seeking

opportunities to enhance skills and knowledge.

9. **Treating staff as Family :** Team leaders shall be a fatherly figure to the team members giving them a comfort of the family. But in case of showing any indiscipline by anyone, take immediate and stern action to give a message to other team members.

10. **Value for Money :** Everyone shall be clear that money is earned by efficient and hard working. Therefore, there shall be optimum utilisation of money in all respects. It does not mean one should be miser. The team leader has also to follow and demonstrate it to the team members to inculcate the habit in them.

Apart from the above commandments I strongly suggest to follow the following advice from some of the most successful personalities of our time:

1. "If four things are followed - having a great aim, acquiring knowledge, hard work and perseverance - then anything can be achieved."

   Bharat Ratna Dr. A.P.J. Abdul Kalam

2. "Take up one idea. Make that one idea your life- think of it, dream of it, live on that idea...This is the way to success."

   Swami Vivekananda – Maker of Modern India

3. "Success can come to you by courageous devotion to the task lying in front of you."

   Noble Laureate Sir C.V. Raman

4. "If you work with determination and with perfection, success will follow."

   Padma Vibhushan E Sreedharan

5. "My success will not depend on what A or B thinks of me. My success will be what I make of my work."

   Padma Bhushan Dr. Homi J Bhabha

You must try to be vigilant and learn as much as you can out of school, college and university, as you are there for a very short period. This education and experience gained will help you throughout your life.

I hope you have enjoyed reading my life story as much as I have enjoyed writing it!

APPENDIX 1

Historical Dates

07-06-1942 : Born in Sialkot, West Pakistan

1947 : Migrated from Sialkot, Pakistan to India.

Yearwise Education and Professional Details

1948 : Admitted in Primary School under the tree with Pandit Ji at Aligarh and stayed till passing 5th Standard

07-06-1952 : Admitted in 6th Standard in Dharam Samaj Inter College, Aligarh

16-06-1957 : Passed High school from Aligarh

30-04-1958 : Passed Qualifying exam of Delhi University

09-12-1961 : Passed B.Sc. from Delhi University

15-01-1962 to
02-07-1962 : Worked as a Salesman for the National Patrika Subscription Agency, New Delhi.

19-07-1962 to
18-02-1963 : Worked as Technical Supervisor at Central Research Institute, Kasauli, Himachal Pradesh

29-06-1963 : Left for the United Kingdom

07-03-1964 : Taken Financial Guarantee from Shri P.N. Anand Under Secretary, Ministry of Health, Government of India, New Delhi

June 1965 : Admitted in B.Sc. Hons. (Chemical Engineering) at Glamorgan College of Technology, Wales, UK

09-12-1968 : Completed B.Sc. Hons. (Chemical Engineering), Wales, UK

July 1969 Admitted in M.Sc. (Chemical Engineering), University of Wales, Swansea

July 1970 : Awarded M.Sc. (Chemical Engineering) and Joined for Ph.D.

July 1972	:	Awarded Ph.D. in Chemical Engineering by University of Wales, UK
10-09-1977	:	Elected an Associate Member of the Indian Institute of Chemical Engineers
25-03-1989	:	Elected member of the Indian Institute of Chemical Engineers.

APPENDIX 2

Details of Visit to Foreign Countries

Sr. No.	Date of Visit	Cities/Countries Visited
1	17-08-1963	London
2	22-09-1968	London
3	12-08-1969	The Netherlands
4	28-08-1969	France
5	30-08-1969	Switzerland
6	02-01-1970	London
7	04-03-1971	London
8	29-04-1974	London
9	22-06-1974	London
10	30-05-1982	London
11	24-08-1984	London
12	02-06-1985	London, Italy, Switzerland, The Netherlands and France
13	09-07-1996	Hong Kong

14	30-04-1996	UK
15	30-09-1996	Switzerland
16	08-07-1998	South Korea
17	29-02-2000	USA
18	21-04-2009	China
19	24-05-2010	Turkey and UK
20	02-05-2011	China
21	27-11-2014	China
22	21-10-2015	Bhutan
23	06-04-2016	Bhutan
24	16-10-2016	Bangkok, Indonesia, Egypt and Jordan

APPENDIX 3

Industries Set-Up

The following companies are owned by Dr. Shingari's family, supported by his wife Dr. (Mrs.) Kiran Shingari and two sons Mr. Gaurav Shingari and Mr. Amar Shingari. It is a family business till date.

Companies at GIDC Industrial Estate, Vadodara

1. **1972:** Chromatography & Instruments Company Manufacturing Unit at Plot No. 122
2. **1975:** Chromatography & instruments Manufacturing & Trading Co. Pvt. Ltd., at Plot No. 121
3. **1975:** Chromatography Training Centre Training Centre at Plot no. 121
4. **1982:** Research & Development Centre at 1st Floor of Plot No. 122
5. **1981-1985:** Doctor & Doctor Building No. 1 completed in 1985 at Plot No. 333-334

6. **1984-1985:** Kiran Associate Building No. 2 completed in 1985 at Plot no. 333-334
7. **1990-1991:** Guest House - "Parishram" completed in 1991 at Plot No. 333-334

Companies at Surya Kiran complex, Deonghat, Solan, Himachal Pradesh

1. **1993:** Precision Scientific Instruments
2. **1999:** Himachal Instrumentation Pvt. Ltd. Closed on **30.09.2003**
3. **2004:** Chromatography & Analysers Company Closed on **30.09.2013**

APPENDIX 4

Awards and scholarships

IIW INDIA

THE INDIAN INSTITUTE OF WELDING
(A Member Society of The International Institute of Welding)

3A, Dr. U. N. Brahmachari Street, Kolkata - 700 017, INDIA

ESAB India Award

is presented to

M. K. Singari

for the Best Technical Paper
across all categories presented at the
National Welding Seminar, 2013 at Bangalore.

Dated: 9th April, 2014

President

भारतीय स्टेट बैंक
State Bank Of India
(02219) KALPAKKAM
6TH AVENUE
DAE TOWNSHIP KALPAKKAM, KANCHEEPURAM, TN 603102

1 4 0 5 2 0 1 4

PAY Dr. M. K. Shingari OR ORDER

RUPEES Four thousand only

₹ 4000/-

10912121120

VALID FOR Rs. 5.00 Lacs & UNDER

Prefix :
0523600001

MULTI-CITY CHEQUE Payable at Par at All Branches of SBI

SHAJU K ALBERT
Please sign above

⑈153742⑈ 673002095⑆ 001146⑈ 31

Appendix 4

Contact Address :
29/31,Ujagar Industrial Estate
W.T.P Marg, Deonar, Mumbai 400 088
Tel: 09967061333 Email: iaia@rediffmail.com

Dr. M.K. Shingari
Managing Director
Chromatography Instruments Company
121- 122, GIDC, Makarpura Industrial Estate
Makarpura, Baroda - 390 010

Dear Dr. Shingari

IAIA Life Time Achievement Award

The Indian Analytical Instruments Association (IAIA) has decided to recognize and honor the pioneering efforts. of veterans in analytical instrument industry in India. We have decided to give the awards in the following three segments:

- *Pioneering the local manufacturing segment of analytical instruments*
- *Pioneering the distribution channel for overseas manufacturers*
- *Pioneer in being an individual having contributed significantly in serving the analytical instrument industry*

In recognition of your design and manufacturing Gas Chromatograph in sixties and establishing CIC as a popular brand for Gas Chromatograph in India and for your commitment for over four decades in manufacturing various other analytical instruments, the executive committee of IAIA is very proud to honor you with

Life Time Achievement Award

The award distribution will take place in the presence of the fraternity of instrument industry, customers and a large number of international visitors, at a special function organized in the evening of Tuesday, September 29, 2009 at the Hitex Exhibition Centre, Hyderabad in the backdrop of Analytica Anacon India 2009 International Trade fair and Conference.

We invite you to be present at the function to accept the award. The function will also include a cultural program and end with cocktails and dinner. We shall send you soon more information about the event.

Please provide us your detailed biodata and a high resolution photograph for including in the souvenir. Should you like to see the details of previous awardees you may visit our web site www.iaia.org.in. We would be very pleased to receive a brief confirmation from you to iaia@rediffmail.com acknowledging the mail.

With kind regards

Mumbai
Sep.1, 2009

Dr.G.Ramakrishnan
President

S.Thyagarajan
Vice President

Indian Analytical Instruments Association (IAIA) - Executive Committee

President	Vice Presidents	Committee Members	Treasurer	Advisors	Secretary
G. Ramakrishnan	S. Thyagarajan Ashes Ganguly	Prashant Shetkar C. Ravindranath Vipul Chhatbar	C.S Shetty	S S Bapat V S Rajan Nitin Kahhin	Gautam Rajan

GLAMORGAN EDUCATION COMMITTEE

Glamorgan College of Technology
Treforest

This is to Certify that

Mahendnar K. Shingari

was awarded the First Prize donated by

The Imperial Smelting Corporation Ltd.

for meritorious work in the

College Associateship in Chemical Engineering

at the

Second Year stage in session 19 65 to 19 66

Chairman of Governing Body E. G. James

Principal [signature]

Director of Education [signature]

UNIVERSITY COLLEGE OF SWANSEA

SINGLETON PARK
SWANSEA, GLAM.
SA2 8PP
TELEPHONE 25678

JMG/ME

1st October, 1969.

Dear Mr. Shingari,

On the recommendation of the Head of the Department of Chemical Engineering, I am now writing to offer you a Research Studentship of the value of £530 plus fees, in the Department of Chemical Engineering for one year from October 1, 1969. The Studentship is normally payable quarterly in advance, but you will receive the first quarters instalment at the end of October.

I will be grateful if you could complete the enclosed personal details form and return it to me as soon as possible.

I will be grateful if you would sign the enclosed copy letter if you accept the appointment and return it to me as soon as possible.

Yours sincerely,

REGISTRAR

Mr. M.K. Shingari,
Research Student,
Division of Chemical Engineering.

Appendix 4

PRIFYSGOL CYMRU
UNIVERSITY OF WALES

COLEG Y BRIFYSGOL ABERTAWE
PARC SINGLETON
ABERTAWE
SA2 8PP

UNIVERSITY COLLEGE OF SWANSEA
SINGLETON PARK
SWANSEA, GLAM.
SA2 8PP

TEL. 0792-25678
COFRESTRYDD ANEURIN DAVIES, M.A. REGISTRAR

All replies should be addressed to the Registrar quoting reference
Dylid anfon pob ateb i'r Cofrestrydd gyda'r llythrennau cyfeir

JMG/CD

19th August, 1970.

Dear Mr. Shingari,

On the recommendation of the Head of the Department of Chemical Engineering, I am now writing to offer you renewal of your Research Studentship in the Department of Chemical Engineering of the value of £900 per annum plus fees, for a further year from October 1, 1970. The Studentship is payable quarterly in advance.

I would be grateful if you would sign and return the enclosed copy letter if you accept the renewal.

Yours sincerely,

Aneurin Davies

Registrar.

Mr. M. K. Shingari,
Research Student,
Chemical Engineering.

PRIFYSGOL CYMRU
UNIVERSITY OF WALES

COLEG Y BRIFYSGOL ABERTAWE
PARC SINGLETON
ABERTAWE
SA2 8PP

UNIVERSITY COLLEGE OF SWANSEA
SINGLETON PARK
SWANSEA, GLAM.
SA2 8PP

TEL. 0792-25678
COFRESTRYDD ANEURIN DAVIES, M.A. REGISTRAR

All replies should be addressed to the Registrar quoting reference
Dylid anfon pob ateb i'r Cofrestrydd gyda'r llythrennau cyfeir

DHA/RE(B.8035)

November 11, 1970.

Dear Mr. Shingari,

Student Demonstrators and Tutorial Assistants
Session 1970/71

On the recommendation of Professor Richardson I write to invite you to act as a Student Demonstrator/Tutorial Assistant in the Department of Chemical Engineering for the Session 1970/71.

The remuneration attached to this appointment will be £60 payment of which will be made in instalments by cheque at the end of each term. You will be required to assist in the work of the department to the extent of 4 * hours per week.

There will be a deduction to cover the cost of Industrial Injuries Insurance. If you have not already done so, will you please arrange to obtain a National Insurance Card and hand it in to the salaries section of Registry.

I should be glad to know, in writing that you are willing to accept this appointment.

Yours sincerely,

Aneurin Davies

REGISTRAR.

* (You have been assigned by the department 6 hours per week for the Michaelmas and Lent Terms only).

Mr. M.K. Shingari,
Department of Chemical Engineering.

PRIFYSGOL CYMRU
UNIVERSITY OF WALES

COLEG Y BRIFYSGOL ABERTAWE
PARC SINGLETON
ABERTAWE
SA2 8PP

UNIVERSITY COLLEGE OF SWANSEA
SINGLETON PARK
SWANSEA, GLAM.
SA2 8PP

TEL. 0792-25678

COFRESTRYDD ANEURIN DAVIES, M.A. REGISTRAR

All replies should be addressed to the Registrar quoting reference
Dylid anfon pob ateb i'r Cofrestrydd gyda'r llythrennau cyfair JMG/SD.

20 July, 1971.

Dear Mr. Shingari,

On the recommendation of the Head of the Department of Chemical Engineering, I am now writing to offer you renewal of your Research Studentship in the Department of Chemical Engineering of the value of £900 per annum plus fees, for a further year from October 1, 1971. The Studentship is payable quarterly in advance.

I would be grateful if you would sign and return the enclosed copy letter if you accept the renewal.

Yours sincerely,

Registrar.

Mr. M.K. Shingari,
Research Student,
Department of Chemical Engineering.

Appendix 4

PRIFYSGOL CYMRU
UNIVERSITY OF WALES

COLEG Y BRIFYSGOL ABERTAWE
PARC SINGLETON
ABERTAWE
SA2 8PP

UNIVERSITY COLLEGE OF SWANSEA
SINGLETON PARK
SWANSEA, GLAM.
SA2 8PP

TEL. 0792-25678

COFRESTRYDD ANEURIN DAVIES, M.A. REGISTRAR

All replies should be addressed to the Registrar quoting reference
Dylid anfon pob ateb i'r Cofrestrydd gyda'r llythrennau cyfair JMG/CD

22nd September, 1971.

Dear Mr. Shingari,

I am writing to inform you that it has been decided to increase the value of your Research Studentship in the Department of Chemical Engineering, for the Session 1971/72 from £900 per annum plus fees to £980 per annum plus fees. This increase is to bring the value of your studentship into line with the value of Science Research Council Post Graduate awards, which have recently been increased.

I have arranged for you to receive this quarter's payment at the end of October, otherwise the increase will be paid in your normal quarterly instalments in advance.

I would be grateful if you would sign and return the enclosed copy letter indicating that you accept this amendment.

Yours sincerely,

Aneurin Davies

Registrar.

Mr. M. K. Shingari,
Research Student,
Chemical Engineering.

PRIFYSGOL CYMRU
UNIVERSITY OF WALES

COLEG Y BRIFYSGOL ABERTAWE
PARC SINGLETON
ABERTAWE
SA2 8PP

UNIVERSITY COLLEGE OF SWANSEA
SINGLETON PARK
SWANSEA, GLAM.
SA2 8PP

TEL. 0792-25678

COFRESTRYDD ANEURIN DAVIES, M.A. REGISTRAR

All replies should be addressed to the Registrar quoting reference
Dylid anfon pob ateb i'r Cofrestrydd gyda'r llythrennau cyfair JMG/CD

18th November, 1971.

Dear Mr. Shingari,

I am now writing to inform you that it has been decided to increase the value of your Research Studentship in the Department of Chemical Engineering for the Session 1971/72 from £980 per annum plus fees to £1,045 per annum plus fees. This increase is to bring the value of your Studentship into line with the recent increase in dependance allowances awarded to Postgraduates.

I have arranged for you to receive the back-dated amounts owing to you in your quarterly instalment, which is paid at the end of December,

I would be grateful if you would sign and return the enclosed copy letter if you accept the increase.

Yours sincerely,

Registrar.

Mr. M. K. Shingari,
Research Student,
Chemical Engineering.

Section 12
Closing Remarks

A letter from Gaurav and Amar Shingari, the Torchbearers of Dr. Shingari's Legacy

This Autobiography of our beloved father, Dr. Mahender Kumar Shingari, is a practical guideline for us and especially for the next generations, who otherwise will not realise how bold, leader and visionary their grandfather was, even with his difficult childhood. They will realise that their comfortable life foundation is the result of a very focused, hard-working, honest and fully committed personality. The reality of his journey of 75 years from a mediocre family to an Industrialist will teach them how to plan their goals and what efforts need to be made to achieve them. They will also learn what are the qualities required to be adopted to be a successful person and a good human.

In fact we feel very proud to be the son of such a person who is focused, has highly disciplined lifestyle, true friend, an excellent father, an excellent husband, nature loving and work for the new goals for all of us as well as for the society.

We are very pleased that our Father has trusted and obliged us to be partners in his business. Now, we hold the positions as Directors of Chromatography & Instruments Company Private Limited (CIC Pvt. Ltd.) and Partners of his Proprietary Company, Chromatography and Instruments Company as Partners. We have been working with him for the last 30 years in his companies. He is now gradually transferring the powers (shares of the companies) to us, to make us more responsible, tolerant and managing the power given. These companies have prospered mainly due to his live demonstration of his Teachings and Training for an excellent Team Leader. He has inculcated hard work, high discipline, sincerity, commitment and honesty in us as well as in the entire teams of all companies.

The realisation of facing hardship under some circumstances was inculcated in us by Daddy Ji since our childhood. As one of the examples, we were made to travel unreserved/sleeper class in the trains though He and Mummy Ji used to travel in A/C coach. This helped us to be tough to face any situation and also to make us mix with ordinary public. Similarly, the value of money was taught to us through the lifestyle followed by Daddy during any business travel. As the Managing Director of the company he will not use hotel in case he has to come back within a day from any tour, in fact he will utilise waiting room. Also, he will prefer common mode of transport instead of flight. The money saved through such actions was given to his needy relatives/relations as a financial support. Even today he insists our children to follow the similar lifestyle even though various comfortable means are possible for them to utilise.

He is very much concerned with the welfare of all the staff but does not tolerate any indiscipline even from us. A recent incident is worth mentioning here. The use of mobile phone during duty hours is strictly prohibited as a company policy and known to every staff member. One of the very senior employee was using his mobile when on duty and a strict warning was issued with a penalty of Rs.500/- as it was his first indiscipline act. Though he apologised immediately in writing but at the same time it is worth mentioning that his bonus and increment will be affected by this act of indiscipline. He was also warned that in case of any repetition of indiscipline he will be terminated immediately. This clearly shows that Daddy Ji cannot tolerate any act of indiscipline.

Another recent incident where we learnt the Leadership quality of our Daddy Ji. There was a power failure for around 2 hrs in the company and we requested him to go back home as it was very hot in his office (ambient temperature 42° C). He kept on working in his office and taught us that if a Commander leaves the battlefield, the Soldiers will be demoralised and ultimately War will be lost. This is a big lesson for us!

Dr. Shingari is a great Visionary. His vision for Indigenisation of High-tech Instruments, like Gas Chromatographs and Determinators in **1972** is a true example of **'MAKE IN INDIA'** which is now a Slogan given by Honourable Prime Minister, Shri Narendrabhai Damodardas Modi Ji in **2014**.

We sincerely thank Daddy's friends who have persuaded Him to document his vast practical experience in facing all kinds of ups and downs in the life. We and our families also got inspired from the timely guidance from Those respectable friends.

We are very fortunate and proud to be the trusted sons of Dr. Shingari. May God bless him with Excellent Health, Prosperity and Vitality!

Gaurav Shingari and Amar Shingari

www.ingramcontent.com/pod-product-compliance
Lightning Source LLC
La Vergne TN
LVHW041138150826
845673LV00001B/37

* 9 7 9 8 8 9 4 1 5 9 8 2 9 *